Caring for Those You Love

Caring for Those You Love

*A Guide to Compassionate Care
for the Aged*

Bethany Chaffin

International Standard Book Number
0-88290-270-9

Library of Congress Catalog Card Number
84-63125

Horizon Publishers Catalog and Order Number
4035

Printed and distributed in the
United States of America
by

Horizon
Publishers &
Distributors, Inc.

50 South 500 West
P.O. Box 490
Bountiful, Utah 84010

ACKNOWLEDGMENTS

Everlasting gratitude to Victor Kassel, M.D., who taught me that compassion is nurtured by knowledge and understanding . . .

And deep appreciation to Shirlea Horne, Leanna Watters and Eleanor Savage who shared with me their skills in geriatric nursing . . . and carefully scrutinized the contents of this book for accuracy.

THE BEGINNING . . .

In June of 1976 I took my husband to a geriatric specialist for an intensive physical and psychological examination. A week later, after the test results were in, the doctor called me into his office for a private consultation. I asked my daughter-in-law, the wife of Frank's son by a former marriage, to accompany me. I wanted to remember every word the doctor uttered.

The kindly but candid physician started by discussing the three types of senile dementia though he didn't call it that. He broke me in gently by talking about less serious illnesses that could be treated or arrested. But in the end I learned that my husband had "Alzheimer's" disease.

I had never heard of Alzheimer's disease before that moment, and the name didn't mean much to me. I simply knew that Frank's memory loss was interfering with his life—with our life—and I wanted it cured.

That dream was in vain. Under the cover of optimism I think I knew it all along. Not only is there no cure for Alzheimer's disease: at the present there is no treatment. It is an irreversible, untreatable, ultimately fatal shrinking of the brain that eventually affects all parts of the body. My husband would grow less and less able to handle his own affairs, and—if he lived long enough—he would be reduced to the simplest state of humanity, unable to take care of his basic needs.

9

I listened to the doctor in silence. After a strategic pause, the doctor told me, "You're taking this all too calmly. You have no idea what you are facing."

My daughter-in-law found her voice before I did. "That's going to be so hard on you, Beth," she ventured.

I shrugged my shoulders and pulled myself together. If this was the way it had to be, I would accept it. Frank and I had a good marriage, one based on mutual respect, and we would weather the storm together.

The last word was the catch. Together. When one's spouse has Alzheimer's, there is no togetherness. There is one dependent mate and one who carries total responsibility for all decisions, for spending money, for maintenance, for scheduling—in short, for everything the couple would normally do as a team.

Those years, hard as they were, have passed. Now my husband resides in a nursing home, greatly handicapped in both mind and body. Names completely elude him, past memories dissolve. Even his own identity is lost in the confusion of his brain. He cannot recall what he did for a living or the names of his children. Through the years I witnessed his paranoia, his accusations, the misuse of money and persecution by his family and friends, all of whom thought I didn't understand him.

But, to have him forget me—that has been the hardest blow of all.

Fortunately I have my work. In experiencing personally the frustration of caring for a loved one who is aging and ill, I found I had a strong desire to share what I have learned with the hope that the traumas of some readers will be lightened, that those who deal with the elderly may gain insight into the problems and peculiarities, as well as the rewards, involved in *Caring For Those You Love.*

Bethany Chaffin

CONTENTS

FOREWORD

A silent epidemic stealing its way into the American economy has nothing to do with microbes, contagion, or chemical warfare; yet it is taking a devastating toll. Eventually every home in America might well be affected by the reality of this widespread pestilence for it will savage wallets and destroy minds and bodies.

The carrier of this "disease" is simply old age and its accompanying dependencies. Old age depletes not only the elderly person himself, but also his entire family and his community, and—in time—the economy of the country in which he lives.

Today more than 20 million Americans are 65 years or older. This segment of the population is the fastest growing age group in the country. It is estimated that, in the next fifty years, this age group will increase by more than 150 percent. The year 2030 will see an expansion of the over-60 set to a projected 65 million. Even as early as 1990, experts estimate that it will cost as much as 30 billion dollars a year to institutionalize only a small number of the elderly, the four to five percent of this age group that suffer from Alzheimer's disease and other forms of senile dementia. Loss or severe impairment of mental powers in this age group will require constant supervision.

Although attention is at last being directed toward the elderly and their special problems, little of it has spilled over to their children, a generation that often feels overwhelmed by the three-cornered struggle to help their elderly parents, raise their growing children, and live their own lives.[1]

United States Senator Charles H. Percy, member of the Senate Special Committee on Aging, records that a sudden wave of shoplifting has hit supermarkets and drugstores, often by the one out of every four men and women over 65 who live below the poverty level in this country. And, for 20 million elder Americans, conditions are getting worse, rather than better.

All too often, in a society that dotes on youth and shelves the elderly, we find the indigent aged women living as "shopping-bag ladies," with their worldly possessions tucked into paper bags which they carry everywhere with them as they move from public library to subway station in search of some sort of temporary shelter from the elements. Hard as it is to accept, many of them eke out a bare living as prostitutes, panhandlers, shoplifters, or bottle collectors. This line of activity becomes ingrained as survival skills and, supplemented by hand-outs from Salvation Army kitchens or other charitable organizations, the homeless manage to live from day to day—until that final hour when a policeman or some citizen finds them slumped in an alleyway, dead from exposure, or starvation, or perhaps a mugging, or rape.

The rewards of life should make us recognize old people as members of the clan who have acquired certain knowledge and skills which can be utilized to teach younger people how to live and develop according to family traditions. Human obsolescence should never be considered for our aged citizens, or our own progenitors.

An old American folk tale might give us pause for reflection. Grandmother, with her trembling hands, was sometimes guilty of breaking a bowl when she ate. Angrily her daughter shoved a wooden bowl at the old lady. A young granddaughter asked why Grandmother had to eat from a wooden bowl when the rest of the family ate on china plates. "Because she is old!" snapped her mother. The child thought for a moment, then said, "You must save the bowl when Grandmother dies." "Why?" asked her mother. The child answered, "For when you are old."

In former civilizations, as well as in many countries today, old age was accepted for accumulated wisdom to teach the youth . . . despite their growing eccentricities. They received, in turn, a respect that may be difficult for our modern, youth-oriented society to understand.

In our culture there exists not only a lack of outrage at the plight of many older citizens, but an actual preponderance of sentimental nonsense and deliberate ignorance concerning the realities of old age. The following list of myths about the aged is often adopted as truths.

Most of the aged are disabled.

Eighty-nine percent of all men and women over sixty-five live in the community and are totally self-sufficient. Only 7 percent are confined to their beds or to their homes. Just 4 percent live in institutions.

Most of the elderly suffer from serious mental deterioration and senility.

Intelligence, as measured in tests of comprehension and knowledge, shows little or no decline for the average elderly person. "Mental deterioration rarely occurs among normal older people before the eighties," says Dr. Robert E. Rothenberg. Evidence indicates the ability to think and reason *increases* with age if those faculties are given sufficient use.

Older people cannot cope with change.

They give up jobs, a way of life, move to a different community or into a smaller house. These changes are greater than those faced by many younger men and women.

Most men and women over sixty-five have no sexual interest or activity.

"Approximately 60 percent of married couples remain sexually active to age seventy-five," says gerontologist Edward W. Busse. For many, sexual interest and activity continue into their eighties and beyond. Lessened sexual capacity often is psychological, caused entirely by current beliefs of society. Elderly men and women who would like to continue sexual activity frequently feel that society disapproves, so they stop. "Let *your* biology, not your neighbor's, be your guide," urges one authority.

All older people are alike.

The aging process spans two and three generations. The differences in characteristics and needs are as great between sixty-year-olds and eighty-year-olds as the differences among any other age categories.

Old age is a disease.

No one dies of old age, according to the AMA's Committee on Aging. "There is no such disease," says *Prevention* magazine. "What we do die of is some infection or degeneration of a vital organ. The more we use every muscle, organ and gland—the more we use our minds—the less likely they are to deteriorate."

Physical limitations imply an inability to function.

A disability need not be a handicap. Many older people adjust to biological changes normal to the aging process and continue to function as vital, interesting men and women.[2]

Until we learn to regard old people as human beings with a future as well as a past, these attitudes are not likely to improve the state of the elderly. The lack of a large family network has contributed to the neglect of the elderly in our culture. Our affluent economy and an advancement in medical care have resulted in earlier marriages for the young and longer lives for the old—and seldom do the two meet.

Most of us can become grandparents at 40, or thereabouts, while we are still productive and reasonably healthy. Our children, and certainly our grandchildren, may live in another city, state, or—not inconceivable in our mobile society—another country. We may not feel any real closeness or communication between the generations. Hence, quality relationships based on love, respect, mutual responsibilities, are no longer a part of the lives of many families.

Perhaps only soaring health-care costs, which hit the pocketbook of every tax-paying American, will serve to correct the mistaken concepts under which many of us labor, and force us to form a realistic basis on which to improve the care of the elderly. Providing health care for a person with a chronic illness can be costly, especially in view of rapidly escalating hospital and medical fees, and if the family is not willing or able to cover these expenses, other means must be found. Much of the financial deficit of this country results from the so-called "social welfare" budget which includes the care of the indigent elderly as well as the overburdened Social Security program.

If the budget is already overdrawn, what effect will rapidly increasing numbers of the elderly have on it? According to the philosophy of our time, the government, rather than the family, seems obligated to care for those who are without resources. Until there is a dramatic change in attitude toward senior citizens and their care, it seems obvious that every one of us must continue to foot the bills, no matter how exorbitant, with our tax money.

This book is based on the premise that aging is a family affair, that the ultimate responsibility for elderly people rests on family members and their resources. But, however we elect to care for our aged, compassion is nurtured only by understanding the problems of old age. It is normal to be intolerant when we don't understand a situation or when we view it with limited knowledge. Familiarity with the problems of aging and with possible resources for help, will encourage the power to cope and to have compassion for our loved ones.

With age comes a need for reassurance. Anxiety about being abandoned and fear of isolation are feelings usually caused by the lack of respect the aged face every day, not by the process of aging in itself.[3] Even if we all slow down a bit as we age, there are still many activities the elderly can — and should — perform. These should not be empty hobbies which merely fill in the time between sun-up and sun-down. When one is 60 or 70 or 80, or older, one still feels the need to "work," to put in some time at a productive occupation of sorts where one can feel he is a part of life around him. Only when an aged person becomes so infirm that he cannot "do" anything should we count him off, put him to bed, and assume full-time care.

And, if the person lives long enough, that time will almost surely come.

Currently, millions of Americans act as major caretakers for ill and aging parents, and, surprisingly, "as painful as the job can be, the rewards can be very great indeed."[4]

Normally a crisis tends either to tear a family apart or bind it more closely together. Most of us panic when we face the possibility of caring for an infirm or demented parent or spouse, but despite the anger, guilt, and impatience attendant to these responsibilities, the caretaker is often exposed to the loved one's wry sense of humor and child-like dependence, both of which can be gratifying. In addition, the caretaker may experience a greater feeling of love regardless of the patient's changed personality or ability to function. The type of love may be altered, it is true, but few things in this life are static. Armed with understanding and knowledge derived from family and community resources, the "nurse" can continue to love the elderly family member as a unique and special human being.[5]

This book is dedicated to all of those who, without fanfare or glory, minister to the needs of the elderly infirm and the senile with Christ-like tenderness and compassion. These are they who truly feed his sheep.

"When thou wast young, thou girdedst
thyself, and walkedst whither thou
wouldest: but when thou shalt be old,
thou shalt stretch forth thy hands, and
another shall gird thee, and carry thee."
John 21:18

_____CHAPTER 1

IDENTIFICATION OF THE PROBLEM

To care for the elderly one must be aware that there are wide discrepancies in this age group. Chronological age is hardly a factor for consideration since some people manage well for themselves at an advanced age whereas others are dependent long before retirement years. One lovely lady of 54 considers herself dependent on her children simply because she has never worked and doesn't know how to support herself after a divorce. Another woman, well into her 80s, is rigidly independent, maintaining a fairly comfortable standard of living on a small monthly pension supplemented by income derived from sewing for her neighbors.

Other factors which must be evaluated are an individual's ineptness, mental or physical handicaps, noticeable changes in personality at home or on the job, degree of dependence on others, and level of employability. Some people are able to function quite normally with severe handicaps; others are completely reliant on family for their care because of minor disabilities.

Perhaps the best scale of judgment to apply is equating the psychic, financial, and physical drain on the family of the patient. Senescence, a decline of functioning, is the simplest test of reality when applied to an aging individual.

Most of us have no difficulty recognizing common symptoms of aging: senility, psychosis, physical enfeeblement such as hardening of the arteries, stiffening of the joints or damage to the heart, vision or hearing; but as long as the person's social and physical behavior is fairly "normal," he is usually accepted by his family. However, even maximally favorable living conditions may not hold at bay, indefinitely, the signs of decline, although loving families may be able to stave off taking dramatic steps for a long time.

Problems seem to explode when siblings are forced to explore the emotional and practical hurdles that thwart them in their efforts to support their aging parents. When do they step in and take over for "Dad"? Feeling their own resources start to crumble, many of the elderly resent intrusion in their affairs no matter how innocently help may be offered. One elderly gentleman, sued for an industrial accident, told his son to "stay out of it." If his wife hadn't stepped in and found a good attorney, the man would have lost his entire estate and been impoverished in his declining years because he was confused beyond the point of taking action against his adversaries.

Time to Take Over

The time comes when younger members of the family must make decisions about "Dad." These decisions should be based on answers to the following questions: (1) How much risk am I willing for my parent to take? (2) Can I distinguish inconvenience from jeopardy? (3) Is there an increased degree of disability? (4) What does the doctor say after a complete diagnostic examination of the patient? (5) How much potential is there for rehabilitation? (6) Does the patient need more care than he is receiving?[6]

No one enjoys the trauma that results from feeling helpless, from the fear of becoming a burden on the rest of the family, or—worse—being exiled from them. Yet deterioration is heart-breaking to witness, and when a child notes such signs as forgetfulness, increasing frailty, or progressive illness, his natural inclination is to want to do something about "Dad's suffering." Sometimes we think "Dad" has nothing to gain by enduring his difficulties and we simply want to make life easier for him.

"Dad" is taken into the home—a first mistake, unless the situation has been carefully assessed. The older person may often be irritated beyond control by noisy, quarreling children, and the normal activity of a growing family. And the family's increased anxiety over "Dad's" infirmities may send "Dad" into the grave before his time.

What, then, is the wisest course of action? If the parent's disabilities are such that he can function more or less independently, with someone coming in to shop and clean once a week, he will probably be happier in his own place.

"With the increased availability of home-delivered meals, home medical care and housekeeping assistance from community and other agencies, the majority of us will be able to remain in our own homes as long as we wish."[7] On the other hand, if the parent forgets to eat, burns himself on the stove when he is cooking, or neglects to take his medicine as prescribed, perhaps he should—for his own good—be uprooted from familiar surroundings and taken into a more sheltered atmosphere.

Assess Patient Needs

A generalized checklist may be helpful to assess patient needs.

Psychological-Emotional State

Psychiatric disorder increases with age so that people over 65 have a high rate of psychological and emotional illnesses.[8] Common sense may prevail in assessing these needs, but since offspring are often unable to be objective about their parents, professional opinion should be sought if there are any questions about a parent's mental health.

Physical State

Only a qualified physician can assess the patient's condition. An examination by a medical doctor specializing in diseases of the aging is a good investment. Make certain you understand his findings, even if you must insist on an extra consultation, so you can ask questions without the presence of the patient.

Functional State

In day-to-day activities such as diet, shopping, bathing, dressing, and cooking, how does your parent fare? Does he take his medicine as prescribed, pay his bills on time, use the telephone, protect himself against possible danger? These questions are answered only by careful observation over a period of time spent with the aging parent. Don't assume Dad's all right if you haven't actually observed his performance in these activities and seen him frequently.

Social State

Is Dad able to stay alone? If he needs help, how much does he need? And is it available? Sometimes children can share their parent's care by alternating days or weeks. The wealthy, of course, can hire help. Others may be able to find resources in the community, or among neighbors or friends.

Financial State

"Financial realities must always be included in the final picture because money—or the lack of it—can be a crucial factor in the recovery process, speeding it up or blocking it completely. When a special diet is called for, or even an adequate diet, elderly convalescents may or may not be able to pay for it. If they cannot, they then may suffer further malnutrition and deterioration."[9]

Furthermore, not everyone can afford rehabilitative aids such as prosthetic devices, physiotherapy, special retraining. To some, these measures are luxuries. Mrs. Jones, for instance, because of a limited monthly income, may never leave her wheelchair again while Mrs. Smith may return to a semi-independent life since she has had the money to pay for recuperative therapy.

Money often rears its ugly head when oldsters must budget stringently. The profile of the average American citizen is not promising. He is probably unemployed and without adequate income to take care of his needs. He has no high school education and, although he receives Social Security, he is without other means such as a private pension. Most of his budget he spends on housing each month, scrimping on food, tobacco, or wine if his budget doesn't balance.

Senator Percy claims that the most severe and pervasive needs for the elderly focus on inadequate income, poor housing, bad nutrition, insufficient medical care, and institutional care and isolation.[10] No wonder finances play such a huge role in the well-being of senior citizens. On a limited scale these problems are being dealt with, but more action is required to insure dignity and purpose in the lives of elderly Americans.

"Most old people feel they can manage because they always have. One old man said he tried to save for a rainy day but couldn't. Now if it rains he expects to drown but he will swim as long as he can. He is representative of the older American; he understands that in the United States the ideal is to work from dawn to dusk and pay your own way. If you can't, you are an embarrassment. Yet that old man worked all his life and contributed his labor to society. He doesn't want 'charity'; just enough to live in his last years with some dignity. So . . . this winter he'll do without heat, eat less often, and on $108 a month he may last till spring. Maybe by spring his advanced society will increase his check. Maybe.

"In the meantime that old man and others like him, all over the country, find no peace, no time for 'retirement.' It is a full-time job to be old and poor."[11]

Biological Changes

Obviously certain biological changes occur as we grow older. Hair grows brittle, thin and dull, gray or white. Skin becomes paler, perhaps blotchy, taking on a parchment-like texture and losing its elasticity. The loss of subcutaneous fat leads to a wrinkled appearance. Sweat glands no longer function as well, and skin may look dry since oil secretions often decrease. More important than these external changes, however, are the slowness, the muscular weakness, and the waning powers which accompany them. Individuals appear to decrease in height. Their posture becomes exaggerated, sometimes developing into a stoop because of muscular weakness and their fear of falling and hurting themselves. A certain advanced shuffle is typical of an aged person's walk, and they become less agile and more restricted in their movements because of reduced efficiency of their cartilage. Changes in the eyes make for less distinct vision, hearing becomes less keen—particularly in men—and the lungs contain a smaller volume of air making breathing less efficient. In general, all cells are less elastic and more fibrous.

With the onset, usually so gradual that the patient does not even consult a doctor, this accumulation of functional losses seems to mark "old age."

On the whole, the digestive system is less affected by aging than most systems of the body, but old folks complain more about digestive functions. Deficiencies of diet are often responsible for illness in old age. Typically, the elderly live alone and have no appetite. Taste buds decrease in number and less saliva and enzymes are secreted, but conservative food preferences and low budgets probably account for most inadequate diets. There is a close relationship between eating habits and emotional state. Old people have been known to starve themselves to death. Depressed and upset, they simply stop eating.

Abnormal Behavior

"It may sound cynical, or even flippant, but . . . when someone's behavior begins to bother someone else, it comes to the attention of private or public social agencies involved in categorizing people as normal or abnormal."[12] But many of the so-called "affective" disorders are reversible and could be treated if brought to the attention of family members who care for their loved ones. The individual may not be able to deal appropriately and realistically with his environment; his relationships with others may be impaired (even with his children); his thoughts may be bizarre, even paranoid, and his actions disorganized. He may be depressed, confused, anxious, or have psychosomatic symptoms. Families can help by offering or securing proper medical or custodial care. Too often, however, these old people live on the periphery of a large community with no nearby family or friends to take an interest.

In that case, alternatives are limited. But there is one strong possibility: "The rate of suicide among old people is high. Social isolation, loss of status, inactivity, poverty, all contribute to the fact that suicide is a major cause of death among the aged."[13]

But while alive, often these patients lose contact with the world to such a degree that TV or books, much less conversation with others, can no longer hold their attention, and they wander aimlessly around the house or yard, not knowing what to do with themselves. Unless closely supervised, they frequently become lost, unable to recall either their name or address. If they are fortunate, some sympathetic soul may get in touch with the local police who know how to handle these cases. If not, they are likely to wander into life-threatening situations.

For many months I'd noticed that my husband had lost interest in reading and TV. A deeply spiritual man, interested in the wonders of the world, he customarily sat in front of the television set each evening with a copy of the scriptures or *National Geographic* in his lap. Now instead of reading or viewing the news, he wandered around the house.

About that time Ferrante and Tiechter, a popular piano duo, came to town for a performance, and throwing caution to the wind, I splurged on two tickets, tucked my husband into the car and away we went, anticipating a good evening's entertainment. I felt he needed the stimulation good music brings, and I needed to get out of the house, among other people.

I enjoyed the concert to such an extent that not until intermission did I notice that my husband was almost totally inattentive. He sat quietly enough in his never-never land, but I could tell he wasn't listening. He even dozed at intervals.

Afterwards I asked if he had enjoyed the concert. "Y-Yes," he answered guardedly, adding, "but it was too l-long." He had merely endured, not enjoyed.

We repeated the experiment with the Harlem Globe Trotters . . . with the same result. Anyone who could ignore the Harlem Globe Trotters, I decided, might better stay at home. So for the next months we simply sat in our livingroom alone each evening. Our children seldom visited us and we had long since lost contact with friends. We were an island unto ourselves. We went only to church and to the grocery store, and even these simple ventures into the world were frustrating because my husband became critical and restless and this made concentration impossible for me.

Frank could not be left alone but I had difficulty trying to make his family realize this. Though he had a son living nearby, and a number of grandchildren, it seemed a chore for them to watch their dad. The one time I left him with his son for the evening, he and his wife went out to dinner with friends! When I called to check on Frank, he was confused and alone with the kids. I hopped into the car and went to pick him up.

A life-long church member, Frank became so restless in services that he was disruptive. "I d-don't belong h-here" or "I c-can't follow w-what they're saying" indicated that he didn't know what was going on and it was terribly confusing to him.

Finally our recreational schedule was limited to walks around the neighborhood, which he seemed to tolerate, and an occasional ride in the car, which seemed to tire him out of proportion.

Our horizon became more limited each day. No one ever came to see us and we seldom left the house. I wasn't writing at all, for when I sat down at the typewriter Frank assumed a stance in the doorway and stared until I gave him my complete attention. After six or eight interruptions, I'd give up and we'd go for a walk.

Complete Examination

In identifying the problems of your loved one, the importance of a thorough psychological and medical examination cannot be overemphasized. A common diagnosis made by general practitioners is to label all forgetfulness as hardening of the arteries, or arteriosclerosis. One patient faithfully took prescribed drugs for four years without benefit before his wife insisted he see a geriatrician, a specialist in diseases of the aging. After extensive tests and a physical examination, the man was diagnosed as a victim of Alzheimer's disease for which there is no treatment. No amount of pills could have helped the man, yet he was subjected to treatment, which, though probably harmless, was anything but helpful . . . plus diagnosis of his actual problem was delayed by years. In his case it made no difference: Alzheimer's takes its toll without mercy, regardless of care, but what if the man had had cancer or Parkinson's in which time is a decided factor?

Many organic conditions can mimic the symptoms of Alzheimer's disease: memory loss, disorientation, and confusion. Among them are strokes, heart attacks, diabetes, infections, tumors, and malnutrition as well as overmedication, the scourge of the elderly who often seek a pill to cure every pain.

Dr. Victor Kassel, geriatrician, Salt Lake City, Utah, writes: "Many physicians and most lay people believe that hardening of the arteries (arteriosclerosis) is responsible for most instances of senility. It is assumed that the arteries in the brain become narrowed by fat and calcium deposits, which result in less blood reaching the brain and an impoverished nutrition. The senility thus is considered secondary to the circulatory deficiency.

"During the past 15 years, autopsy examinations by British geropathologists have shown that the association of cerebral arteriosclerosis with senility is incorrect. Rather, the cause is arterial blood vessel disease in the neck and below the head. Thus, the true cause of the 20% of senility cases alleged as cerebral arteriosclerosis are diseases outside the brain. Small parts of the brain are destroyed by foreign matter broken off from the blood vessels' walls and this material flows up to the brain to destroy the brain tissue. It is correctly called 'multi-infarct dementia' (M.I.D.).

"The cause is not hardening of the arteries of the brain (cerebral arteriosclerosis). Medicine, vitamins, and herbs touted to improve this so-called circulatory deficiency are worthless."[14]

In the event of stroke, or heart attacks and fractures, the potential for correction of resultant disabilities should be considered. Therapy can often be provided near the patient's

home in hospitals or other medical facilities. However, not
all physicians feel that the elderly patient is a suitable re-
cipient for such services, and sometimes the patient's family
does not know enough about their loved one's condition to
press the issue. The patient's own determination and the
speed with which therapy is pursued are often critical factors
for success.

Physical Problems

A patient with physical problems often appears different
to the average eye, and because his handicap slows him
down, his caretakers may feel he can't do things for himself—
like dressing, for instance. Given enough time, a handicapped
individual can perform many tasks, and perhaps should, so
that his life will continue much as it did before his illness.
The answer to this problem is determined by how well the
patient is dealing with his handicap. Let the patient do as
much for himself as he can, but be there in case he needs a
helping hand . . . and someone who cares. "Human contact is
just as essential to handicapped people as to normal ones,
and just as essential to the old as to the young."[15]
In assessing the elderly patient's condition, family members should always ask the physician for sufficient knowledge
about the patient's prognosis so that they feel well-informed.
The doctor's diagnosis should be explained in terms of how it
affects the patient, what changes in his routine are required,
and what danger signs should be watched for. A doctor should
explain the basis for this recommendation, whether it in-
volves home care, surgery, or medical treatment. No competent physician will hesitate to give an explanation, nor will
he be insulted if you ask for it. The professional who seems
too busy to answer questions should be avoided if possible.
Professional opinion should be a helpful support in your
decision-making, but you should know your parent or spouse
better than any outsider, no matter how professional. However, in this day and age, with the divided family so common,
some children simply do not know their parents, and this
must be taken into consideration. Too, no matter how devoted,
children are sometimes reluctant to admit that their parent

is crumbling. Denial in the face of overwhelming medical evidence is not unheard of.

The burden of decision-making must rest upon those who are competent, interested, and informed. Before reaching a decision, explore all possibilities. If you are fully employed and no one is home to care for an aging parent, it is foolhardy to yank your father who needs constant (24-hour-a-day) attention from his condominium and place him in an environment where he will be more confused and still not have the care his condition requires.

Nursing Homes

Nursing homes, and other boarding facilities, provide trained personnel who work eight-hour shifts around the clock to administer to the needs of custodial patients. (See later chapter to judge the merits of such institutions.) To give a needy patient part-time care is doing him a disservice no matter how much "love" you may feel for him. Others may be able to give him better care.

An observation may suffice for allaying any fears about the coldness of nursing-care facilities. A daughter-in-law placed her hands on her hips after visiting her husband's father in a rest home one Sunday. "Well, they may take good care of him physically," she exploded, "but they don't give him any love." On investigation, I learned that just before her visit the patient had defecated in the closet and a young orderly, gagging while trying to subdue his sense of smell, cleaned up the mess without objection. Shoes and other items of apparel on the floor were swiftly wiped off, then cleaned thoroughly. A few minutes later he was bathing the patient, an elderly man in advanced stages of senility. I overheard their conversation. "Now, Johnny, let's soap your foot. That's right, lift it up and let me wash it. Good! Now the other one."

I'd heard enough. If that isn't love, what is? To clean up human waste, then treat the patient with dignity and respect must be the highest order of love . . . and devotion. People who work in rest homes have an extra dimension of patience and understanding. The few who are not naturally equipped to cope with this kind of work do not last long.

"Inasmuch as ye have done it
unto one of the least of these . . .
ye have done it unto me."
Matthew 25:40

CHAPTER 2

UNDERSTANDING TREATMENT

Not all cases of impending age resemble the pattern of gradual but definite enfeeblement, admission to a nursing home, and senile deterioration or psychotic breakdowns. A growing community of the over-sixty-five set, with increasing numbers of those in the seventies and eighties, fend for themselves, trying to maintain their independence as long as possible. And they should, for we've all heard stories of men who retired so they could "enjoy life," only to die after a few months of enforced leisure. Most of us thrive on routine. A man who has worked all of his life in industry, etc., or a woman who has kept house for forty years, will not take kindly to being put on the shelf with nothing to do but amuse themselves. Chances are, they will be anything but amused. The hours will hang heavy on their hands, and they will, as some put it, "Look forward to death."

Eventually even self-sufficient oldsters will need assistance. Although they often become impatient or angry with their own impotence in dealing with the affairs of the world, as they have known it, at times they display a wry sense of humor or insight which is valuable to the caretaker.

One lady tried to reassure her husband of her love so that he would feel secure in his growing infirmity. She really poured it on. "I love you, dear. Let me protect you from the frustration of growing old. Nothing matters except our love, and that won't change, regardless of your age or disability."

Her husband scrutinized her with a serious scowl. She fully expected him to reciprocate by exchanging some sweet sentiment, but he surprised her. "You might *love* me," he answered, "but you don't *like* me very much!"

All families who have disabled members must face certain situations, but they can either grow more firmly unified as a family or they can let conditions initiate a crisis. This particular wife chose to overlook her husband's bitter remark, and to pacify him, if she could. "No," she answered gently. "I love you." Then with a smile, "Sometimes I even like you, too." This brought a tiny smile to her husband's lips and made her feel as if she had accomplished a minor miracle.

Changes in Personality

Situations which might precipitate a crisis can be turned to an advantage by a thoughtful caretaker. One old gentleman had started to hallucinate. To him, the spiders that covered the wall in his bedroom were as real as any encountered in the woods on a summer's stroll. He screamed, "Take them away! Get them off my wall!" His perceptive daughter touched him on the arm. "It's O.K. now, Dad. I just brushed them all out the window." The man calmed down immediately as he stared at his daughter with newfound respect. She had saved him. No amount of logic could have dislodged the insects, but her cool, collected reassurance settled the matter.

Some people seem to experience dramatic changes in personality as they grow older, yet more than one authority claims that the patient's personality quirks merely become more pronounced, as if he says to himself, "Well, Joe, you're getting older now and you've got a right to do your own thing." Though many character traits may remain unchanged, a few become exaggerated. For instance, if a person has a short temper or has been easily irritated in the past, with a dementing illness his temper may become explosive. Other patients range in emotions from passive to demanding, or from energetic to apathetic. Fear, dependency, and depression are not unusual ploys of the elderly.

A daughter reports, "Mother was always the cheerful, outgoing person in the family. We knew she was getting forgetful, but now she is surly, she doesn't want to go out anymore, and she refuses to keep herself or the house clean."

From another family: "The worst thing about Dad is his temper. He used to be easygoing. Now he is always hollering over the slightest thing. Last night he told our little son that Alaska is not a state. He yelled at the kid, then stomped out of the room. Then, when I asked him to take a bath, we had a real fight. He insisted he had just taken a bath and he wasn't about to take another!"[16]

Every nursing home attendant can relate stories about frail old men striking out violently at each other over trifles. One patient, ordinarily the mildest of men, made the mistake of directing a blow at a younger patient one day only to be decked for his effort! When his wife visited that evening and saw a bad bruise on his forehead, she was troubled. After the nurse explained the situation, the wife gently teased her husband who couldn't remember the incident. "Now," she said with a smile, "I want you to take it easy, honey. Remember, you're a lover, not a fighter." Perhaps something of the altercation remained in the old man's mind, for he grinned at her. Or maybe her words had only reminded him that he was, after all, still a man!

It would be well to keep in mind that such changes in personality and behavior are beyond the control of the patient. The caretaker must consider this, not act as one son did when his father tried to fend off his son's attempts to shave him. The son promptly hit the old man back! Chastized by someone more conversant with the changes in the old man, the son rebuttaled, "But he socked me four or five times!"

Unusual personality manifestations are not due to any childish desire to have one's own way, but, rather, to subtle changes in the brain which eventually affect the way the patient speaks, his memory, his ability to dress and feed himself and his coherence. These abilities will fluctuate from day to day, making the situation a frustrating experience for the caretaker unless he understands what is happening.

Communication skills are frequently the first to go. Problems centering around words, and the ability to think, often plague the elderly and make them appear rebellious or uncooperative. Usually they are neither. They simply do not understand what is expected of them.

I became aware of this when my husband, by nature a quiet, considerate man, started questioning everything I did with a defensive, "I don't know what you want of me!" As an English major I had studied communication most of my life, and I thought my requests were obvious. My words may have been well-chosen, but communication between us was faulty. He couldn't understand the meaning of my words.

Nor could he express himself clearly. Never a verbal man, as his illness wore on he became close-mouthed, refusing to socialize and often leaving the room to wander through the house until guests left. He didn't even have enough social poise to remain at the wedding reception of a son, which was held at our home. I know now that the job of host was too much for him to handle. I didn't realize that then, however, and the confrontation that followed his return is better left unrecorded.

Catastrophic Reactions

Caretakers are advised to avoid any situation which might bring on a catastrophic reaction. A lapse in mental power—or physical for that matter—is frustrating to patients, but avoiding a confrontation should pave the way to smoother relationships. "Strange situations, confusion, groups of people, noise, being asked several questions at once, or being asked to do a task that is difficult . . . can precipitate these reactions."[17] When patients are confronted by these situations they try to place the blame on someone else (usually the caretaker), striking out physically, verbally, or sometimes denying any part in the action.

A catastrophic reaction does not always resemble action taken by a mental patient, however. It may manifest itself as stubbornness, obstinacy or critical behavior. Sometimes the patient merely seems to be overreacting. But whatever appearance his behavior assumes, both he and the caretaker will be better off if such reactions can be avoided. One physician issues the following instructions for caretakers:

1. Don't argue with the patient.
2. Don't try to reason with him.
3. Don't expect anything of him.

Keeping these three rules in mind can avert potentially catastrophic situations.

Communication Skills

You will communicate better with an older person if you:
1. Make sure he hears you.
2. Lower the pitch of your voice.
3. Eliminate distracting noises or activities.
4. Use short words and sentences.
5. Ask only one question at a time.
6. Ask the patient to do only one task at a time, not several.
7. Speak slowly and wait patiently for his response.[18]

Both patient and caretaker will benefit from positive body language. The patient is upset by unspoken messages that indicate the caretaker is tired, impatient, or disgusted with him. Instead, the caretaker should always try to remain calm, pleasant, and supportive, taking the patient's hand or in some other way expressing affection. A direct look will often indicate whether or not the patient is paying attention, and if he isn't, probably the attempt to communicate should be aborted in favor of a later time. Other signals besides words can be utilized. Try pointing, touching, handing him an object or demonstrating an action, and by all means avoid assuming complex reasons for his behavior. Try to imagine what he feels, rather than decipher what he is trying to say.[19]

Waning Coordination

A slow, shuffling gait is a sign that the older patient is suffering from apraxia, the inability to make the arms, legs or fingers do as the brain directs. Besides memory loss, the older patient often experiences the loss of muscle control which leads to difficulty in dressing, bathing, and eating. Usually these patients are unable to learn new ways of doing things, so the best way to cope with their disabilities is to simplify. Buy shoes that slip on, rather than tie; select dresses or shirts that slip over the head, rather than ones with buttons or zippers.

Unless the disability is minimized, this lack of control will convince a person to stop activities he has enjoyed all of his life. A woman may give up knitting, a man his hobby of woodworking because they both feel clumsy, and if they are tense as well, they will be even less capable of performance. Encourage them to do what they enjoy, even though their work may be far from perfect. Make allowances for their disabilities. Research seems to indicate that the busier the body part, the less loss of function, and that includes the brain.

Muscle weakness or stiffness in the joints may further disable a person who does not walk around much. Exercise is important for all patients, the amount and type restricted only by physical disabilities. Specialty books recommend specific exercises for the infirm, even for those confined to bed. Examining such a book to select possible movements for your patient might pay big dividends. Most of us feel better when we are engaged in a regular exercise program. So it is with the infirm.

Falls are perhaps one of the greatest dangers of old age since old bones do not heal as readily as do young ones. When a patient becomes so unsteady on his feet that falls seem probable, provide railings or other support if the patient is expected to get around. A firm hold on his upper arm can give him the necessary confidence to walk from the bedroom to the bathroom so that he can retain at least some degree of normalcy.

Restlessness

Restlessness may be an aspect of aging that friends and family must try to understand. When a patient is well enough to go out to dinner, he may either eat and run or put his coat on and try to leave before dinner is served. This is not a matter of rudeness. The patient's ability to judge time has been lost, and this is frequently one of the early losses in aging. Chastizing him will do no good. Most families simply give up their social lives when a victim becomes this disturbed, but there are subtle ways to modify this type of behavior so that the husband or wife can enjoy an occasional dinner with their grown children.

Remember that the restaurant or house is unfamiliar to the patient, and the atmosphere is probably more noisy or confusing than home. Furthermore, the patient has lost track of time. No wonder he wants to leave! If you can provide some familiar activity that he still enjoys immediately after dinner (or before, if he shows a tendency to want to leave), you may be able to visit with others for a short time.

Restlessness during normal sleeping hours is another matter. I had known my husband suffered from Alzheimer's disease for several years before it took its toll on our sleeping routine. Frank had always been a good sleeper. We used to say that he could sleep when the wind blew because his conscience was clear. Nothing had ever disturbed his rest. But later in his illness, his patterns changed. Sometimes he would awaken several times in one night, sit straight up . . . and scare me half to death.

In order to calm him so he could sleep, I'd get up with him, pace awhile, then fix him some hot chocolate and a piece of toast and talk. Usually he'd return to bed. But before his illness terminated in his being confined to the rest home, he awakened as many as twelve or thirteen times a night. His doctor told me to let him wander, but I couldn't do that. For one thing, he was having trouble finding the bathroom, and for another I was afraid he'd actually leave the house and wander away. The third reason, however, was the most valid: I simply couldn't sleep with him awake and wandering through the house. And so my health suffered along with his.

I recalled the first time his wakeful hours disturbed me. We were spending the summer at our home in the mountains where fresh air and vigorous hikes usually induced deep sleeping patterns. He seemed especially restless one day, but I attributed it to the fact that I was tutoring a group of students who took me away from him for part of each day. He wasn't alone. My grown daughter, home from college for a few weeks, was caring for him. They had always gotten along well, and he felt comfortable with her since he had helped raise her.

We went to bed as usual and I fell immediately asleep. In what seemed like just a moment, he sat up in bed, crying, "Oh, my head, my head!" He clutched at his temples and groaned.

"What is it?" I mumbled, hardly awake.

He couldn't tell me, but when he'd finally settled himself enough to speak, he said, "I think . . . I'm going crazy."

I was shocked. Not at the thought of his going crazy—*I'd* known that for some time—but because *he* knew it. What torment he must feel! I had hoped to shield him from that horrible realization.

I tried to dismiss the thought. "Oh, no, honey. You probably had a nightmare . . . a bad dream."

He shook his head. "No, I'm going crazy." Then he looked at me in the dim moonlight coming through our open window. "Aren't you frightened?"

Wide awake, I took his arm and tried to soothe him. "No, dear, I'm not afraid. You'll be all right. Don't worry. Please," I pleaded with him.

Again he asked, "Aren't you afraid?"

By then I knew it was no dream. He'd had some special manifestation of his condition. Any arguments I could offer would be futile. I turned on the bedside light and sat up with him. "No, Frank, I'm not afraid. You see, the doctor has prepared me. I know what to expect."

He seemed surprised. "You do?"

"Yes. And I can handle it. Don't worry. I'm not afraid and you mustn't be, either. It's just your illness, and I know what to do, so just go back to sleep if you can."

That was the beginning of a series of sleepless nights which progressed into a one-hour down, two-up sort of pattern, pacing the floor until he became brave enough to try to sleep again. I never knew what kind of dreams he had, or if they weren't dreams why the thoughts plagued him especially at night, but whatever it was—whether vague premonition or discomfort in his head—he was right. He was going crazy. Now we both knew it.

Confinement

Later I asked a friend, a Hospice volunteer who had experienced old age in its final hour under many different circumstances, "How long do you think it will be before I . . . have to—before I won't be able to keep him at home?"

She paused before answering. "Within a year, I'd say, at most."

I forgot about our conversation until nine months later when I had to place my husband in a home in Salt Lake City. Meanwhile I had investigated facilities within a 150-mile radius. I selected the one I placed him in as having the best facilities for our needs. It wasn't an easy decision. I had packed and unpacked his clothes three times before I was able to admit him.

I wondered how my friend knew. She hadn't watched us getting out of bed ten or twelve times each night. She hadn't stripped his clothing off when he wet himself simply because he had forgotten how to work the zipper. She hadn't answered the same question ten times in a half hour. She hadn't dealt with faulty convictions which no amount of reason could sway. She hadn't been confined with him, hour after hour, day after day, week after week, hungering for a little intellectual conversation, a time to think without interruption, a bit of culture, or even a good movie.

She hadn't endured outrageous persecution or lifted 175 pounds of dead weight out of the bathtub or tried to bend stiff joints to fit into sleeves or slacks. But she knew. She knew the pattern of illness . . . the difficulties of the caretaker. The frustration. The fatigue. The loneliness.

Now, a year later, I admit that if I had it to do over again, I would keep my husband at home as long as I could because there were moments of reward—few and far apart perhaps— but still, I did the right thing. I kept him with me until his physical needs were such that he required the care of professionals. Then I let him go.

In the nursing home, the attendants sense our ongoing relationship despite the fact that he no longer knows who I am. One young woman said, "You and your husband have such a special relationship. I can feel it between you. He is always better after you've visited him. Most of our patients don't have anyone."

I knew what she meant. Sometimes Frank ignored me, but usually I could bring him around by touching him or kissing him, or simply by talking quietly to him. His brain was dying, I knew, but something else remained. Our spirits, perhaps, or body language. Whatever it was, I was grateful.

Strained Relationships

Joey, an MS patient, was confined to bed. His wife visited him only on Christmas and his birthday, and after those visits Joey was upset for days. His wife had kept him home too long, out of a sense of duty, until she hated the man and the burden he'd become. And Joey returned her hatred, for he realized his own inadequacies. Their twice-a-year visits were filled with loud arguments and cursing until the staff dreaded to see those holidays come around.

Usually such behavior is beyond the control of the patient, and the caretaker would do well to remember that. However, the patient's abilities may differ from day to day, causing even more frustration, so that families hardly know what to expect from visit to visit.

A persecution complex is common in patients with brain damage. Usually they will accuse those nearest and dearest to them of stealing their purse or usurping their estate, without any tangible evidence. Their accusations are so convincing that those around him begin to wonder what they've done to deserve such rancor.

About a year and a half before Frank's admission to a rest home I was served divorce papers which included a restraining order forcing me to turn over the business checkbook plus other records for examination. The summons server arrived at our home late at night after we'd spent a lovely holiday season with our children, and I thought we were in a state of serenity that would last forever. As soon as I scanned the papers, I presented them to Frank.

"Do you know what you've done, Frank?"

The confusion on his face was answer enough. "I-I d-don't know anything a-about this," he stammered, examining his signature. It was his, all right. There was no doubt about the tiny, upright letters.

"I'm afraid you do, Frank. This is your signature."

A frown creased his widening forehead above troubled eyes as he handed the documents back to me. "I-I didn't m-mean anything like th-this," he protested.

My future was threatened. The papers stated that the house would be Frank's, that I was capable of supporting myself, and there would be no alimony. The lawyers had thought of everything. I was to be thrown out on the street.

I didn't complete the story for a few days, but right from the start I knew this was no doing of Frank's. The accusations were impossible for him to utter since by this time his speech was greatly affected. And he couldn't have found his way to an attorney by himself.

As I suspected, he'd had help. In a state of depression fostered by paranoia, Frank appealed to his son and because the man had not been close enough to his father to recognize signs of mental illness, he took him to the lawyer's and helped to translate what he thought were his dad's wishes. The attorney, sensing a fat fee, took it from there.

The very night the papers were served, Frank denied signing them, and the next day he declared this wasn't what he wanted. We made an appointment with the attorney who treated me like a conniving gold digger and embarrassed and maligned me for several hours while we discussed the disposition of the trust which Frank had revoked.

In the final analysis, the trust was reinstated about the same as the original. The lawyer came as close to an apology as he could, and the only harm from the whole mess was the legal fee of $1000 and a feeling inside me that no one in the whole world could be trusted. Probably this was a valuable experience, for I learned how my husband must feel from time to time—that everyone was against him, and that he was being robbed of everything he'd worked for all his life!

Actually it was I who had insisted on the trust in the first place, and I had worked diligently on the properties so that they could be passed on to Frank's sons. If I had wanted to take advantage of an old man, I could have done it a lot earlier . . . and a lot cheaper.

This situation is perhaps not too exaggerated as an example of paranoia in the elderly. They usually bite the hand that feeds them, and the caretaker would be well advised to be wary.

Cooperation with Caretakers

In the final stages of a dementing illness, the brain is so disabled that the patient will be confined to bed, unable to care for himself or to communicate. Ultimately he will need twenty-four-hour-a-day nursing care, and this may mean that he must be admitted to an institution.

Nursing homes and other custodial accommodations have been criticized by many unfamiliar with the care they give old people. In truth, the patient's family and the patient himself usually receive the kind of care they expect. Attendants are human, and although most of them are devoted to the seniors in their care, there is no doubt that both patient and family cause a great deal of unnecessary distress. A son approaching his father noticed that the old man was not wearing his glasses. He stormed to the nurses' station and demanded that they find them on the spot. The busy attendants, put on the defensive, were unable to locate the missing spectacles, and the rest of the afternoon flew into a turmoil. Both father and son were upset, and so were the nurses. As the son left the home, he muttered something about inefficiency. They couldn't even keep track of his father's glasses!

More to the point was the fact that the father, in less than two weeks' time, had misplaced two pairs of glasses, and the head nurse was unwilling to let him have access to the third pair for fear he would lose them as well. They were kept in a box where she could get her hands on them when the patient could be watched to make sure he kept them on his face. Unfortunately, the head nurse was off the floor at the time of the son's visit.

Contrast this with another scene: same subject, different characters. When the wife of the elderly gentleman came to visit, she greeted him warmly, conversed with him for a few minutes, then asked, "Would you like to wear your glasses while I'm here?" The old man nodded, so she walked to the nurses' station, reached over into the box where they were stored and remarked to the nurse that she would be responsible for the glasses, and when she left she would return them.

During her visit the patient wore the glasses, enjoyed the even tenor of their conversation, and gave up the glasses for safe keeping when the wife started to leave. The wife, of course, had the advantage: she had searched for her husband's glasses thousands of times, and she appreciated the attendants' problem in trying to keep track of the blasted things!

A grandson of this same man lived only a few blocks away, but he hadn't seen his grandfather for some time. When the grandmother tried to explain her husband's waning powers, the young man glowered at her, snarling sarcastically, "Well, give him *some* credit!" Helpless to cope with his misdirected anger, the woman tried to further describe her husband's illness, but the young man was unwilling to listen, preferring to believe, instead, that she was diminishing his grandfather. The irony of this whole episode lies in the fact that the grandson had been working in a hospital for several years, took great pride in his knowledge of things medical, and planned to become a doctor!

Needless to say, the conversation upset the patient the wife had tried to protect. Although he couldn't understand what was going on, he felt the hostility between two people that he loved, so the wife gave in rather than distress her husband further. The young man would learn the facts about Alzheimer's in the years ahead . . . perhaps as a victim!

Mental patients, and this often includes the elderly, require a calm, structured environment and routine . . . and constant supervision. Those who care for them must recognize this fact and plan accordingly. If your home cannot provide this kind of atmosphere, then you'll be doing your aging parent a disservice if you take him into it. Caretakers must have the patience to answer endless questions quietly, without irritation, to cope with cleaning up after the patient, giving him baths and dressing him when he can no longer perform those tasks for himself, feeding him, listening to him time after time when he cannot express himself, and in all likelihood, bearing the brunt of his frustrated anger. All of these tasks take physical strength and emotional objectivity, as well as time. Be certain that you are willing to expend most of your energy in this direction before you offer to take "Dad" into your home. It may be that he needs the care of professionals who work eight-hour shifts and have developed the objectivity to deal with demanding patients.

On the other hand, there are alternatives to both home care and care provided by a custodial facility. Sometimes the patient needs full-time care only for a short time—until he heals from an accident or a broken leg, for instance. When he recovers, he can again assume his independence. Also, some old people manage very well for a time with occasional outside help: a visiting nurse or housekeeper, a social worker or health aide.

A later chapter will discuss these and other options in more detail. The right choice for your loved one can be made only after you examine all the possibilities and assess your patient's needs.

*"And he shall be ... a restorer of thy
life, and a nourisher of thine old age."*
Ruth 4:15

CARING FOR PHYSICAL NEEDS

The field of geriatric medicine has become a new focal point of interest in research, a fact which is encouraging since many of us will reach our eighth or ninth decades. The process of aging has always been a mystery, but it is now becoming a mystery that can be unraveled a step at a time. Naturally, most of the progress in solving this puzzle will be performed by experts in the field, but we are beginning to realize that not only are people living longer, they are living better — or at least they can, with a little help.

Often diseases can be prevented if they are dealt with early enough in their development. A lot of unnecessary suffering and pain can be eliminated if we refuse to attribute every ache and pain an oldster may have to "old age." Symptoms should not be ignored. Nutrition should be studied as well as exercise and proper social interaction to determine whether the aging person is receiving the best in care so that he can remain independent and self-reliant as the years pass. Prevention of illness should include vaccination for flu and pneumonia and regular screening for detection of anemia, diabetes, hypertension, rectal and breast cancer, and other related diseases.[20] Old age should not be considered a time of life to be stoically endured. Behavioral psychologist B. F. Skinner suggests, "Attack old age as a problem to be solved,"[21] and "New research undermines the old notion that ... decline is a natural, inevitable feature of old age."[22]

Scientists are learning to retard the aging of the brain as well as the body because the changes we have come to expect, they say, need not affect the elderly to the degree that they seem to do. Anyone who is in reasonably good health should expect to enjoy life well into his eighties. The way to keep alert—and functional—is to stay active, interested, and challenged by life. Many senior citizen centers report that old folks are dancing three and four times a week . . . and loving every minute of it.

Why do some older citizens remain active while others retreat into a shell and refuse to partake of life? The answer seems to be activity, and an interest in preserving good health. The elderly need to eat right, get regular exercise, keep chronic problems like high blood pressure under control, and keep a record of all medications they take.

Furthermore, those of us who have loved ones who are growing older can play an important role in making them feel vital and alive. We should not—though we often do—assign them the part of an aging, failing, incompetent human being. Being human, they usually play the role we assign to them. The key to all of this is to encourage as much activity and independence as the person can tolerate . . . and enjoy. When one gives up, he dies. The mind exerts a great influence on physical health.

Good Habits

Where do we start, you may ask. If you are responsible for an aging relative or friend, probably the first step is to see that he receives proper nutrition, and this should include controlled doses of vitamins. A study in Great Britain showed significant results after patients were given nutritional supplements. It seems that chronic vitamin deficiency could prove to be one of the simplest remedial treatments for problems incurred by the aged.[23] Definite improvement in only one year was found in the following areas: aging process, mental and physical health, neuropathies, cardiac failure, gastro-intestinal disease, infections, mouth ulcers and painful dentures.

Basic health rules should be followed religiously by the elderly, but if they cannot see to do this themselves they may have to be supervised. See to it that they practice seven principles for maintaining good health.

1. Eat regularly and not between meals.
2. Eat breakfast.
3. Get seven to eight hours of sleep each night.
4. Keep a normal weight.
5. Refrain from smoking.
6. Drink moderately, if at all.
7. Exercise regularly.[24]

Good health can be effectively and inexpensively preserved if these rules are followed. After all, it makes sense to prevent disease rather than to treat it.

It is estimated that one-half to two-thirds of the deaths of the elderly in America are related to malnutrition, and malnutrition is often the cause of so-called senility. But this can be reversed if the patient receives proper nutrients in sufficient quantities. An older person who has decided not to eat, however, will need some persuasion. The hot lunch program sponsored by the federal government has probably done as much to encourage people over 65 to eat as anything, because in this program the seniors meet together several times a week for food and for company. Those in charge make certain that the food is well-prepared and palatable and that sociability is encouraged.

You can take a lesson from this example at home. Make mealtime a pleasurable experience. Serve small, colorful portions on pretty dishes (not in a wooden bowl!) and set them on an attractive tablecloth. Or, if the patient must eat in his room, use a nice tray with attention to the same details. Tempt him with goodies if he finishes his meal and praise him profusely when he cleans up his plate. Even the elderly respond to flattery.

Because old people often have lost their natural teeth, or may have dentures which are ill-fitting or uncomfortable, make sure that the food you serve is soft enough for him to chew, or cut it in small pieces so that he can masticate it easily. And keep the conversation pleasant and calm. Don't pick on mealtime to chastize your children, for instance. This may upset Grandpa to the point where food doesn't appeal to him. And if he should spill or break a dish, minimize the event. A mess or a broken dish is nothing compared to the patient's health.

If by chance the older person, or couple, still lives in their original home, then Meals on Wheels, a part of the National Nutrition Program for the Elderly, will prepare and deliver one hot meal a day, including special diets, if necessary, for a small fee. Anyone independent enough to live in his own home can usually manage breakfast and lunch; it is the main meal of the day — the hot dinner or supper — that baffles him.

The federal government also publishes two pamphlets helpful for this age group: *Guide for Older Folks* and *Family Food Budgeting*, both available from the United States Printing Office.

Aides for the Disabled

With physical disabilities the caretaker of the patient will learn to contend with what must seem like insurmountable obstacles. In the book, *Caring for the Disabled Patient*, an illustrated guide, the author gives helpful advice about common geriatric problems. The chapter titles illustrate:

Oh, My Achin' Back!
What's Wrong With Me?
My Arm's No Good
Fix My Pillow, Please
I'm Wet!
My Muscles Are Too Weak
Take Me To The Toilet
Did You Say Walk?
I Can't Do It
I'm Tired of TV
Just Leave Me Alone
I Don't Want Any Lunch
Etc.[25]

Sometimes a residence will require alterations to make it more convenient for the patient. Such additions as a ramp

for a wheelchair, railings along the walls to aid
even a red toilet seat to facilitate finding the
these will aid in making the caretaker's tasks l...
and in keeping the patient as independent as possibl...
long as possible. Throw rugs, waxed floors, scalding hot-water
taps and other household niceties may have to be avoided as
long as the patient remains in the house. Simplify as much as
you can; your work will be hard enough as it is.

If your patient has been removed from his own home, try
to include in his room some of his favorite things: an old chair,
a reading lamp, some pictures, a smoking stand, etc., so that he
will feel he has not been dislodged completely.

The older person will often become overly concerned with
his health, particularly if he has nothing else to think about.
Answer his questions as clearly and unemotionally as you can,
being moderately sympathetic but not overly so. Try to assure
him that you understand his feelings and make him as comfortable as you can. If you feel you should, by all means consult
with his doctor (a specialist, preferably) by telephone to determine if there is an emergency. Usually the doctor will
advise you on the best course. Follow his instructions and
deal with the complaint as well as you can.

Most geriatric patients lose control of their bladder or
bowels, or both, at a certain stage of their deterioration.
Medical supply stores handle all kinds of devices and dress-
ings to make your work a little easier. No one likes to clean
up human waste, but with catheters or large diapers the job
is not quite so distasteful, and the patient will feel better if he
does not have to lie or sit in his own excreta. Disposable
diapers have been a boon to those who care for the elderly
as well as to young mothers.

Bowel movements, or the lack of them, seem to dominate
elderly patient's thoughts. Due to lack of exercise, a general
slowing down of the body and activity, and a change in diet,
the bowels may indeed cease to function in a "normal" pattern.
Fecal impaction, one of the most common problems, should
be anticipated and thereby avoided with the use of stool
softeners, stewed prunes, juice, or mineral oil before it becomes a problem. However, if bowel movements grow irregular

and troublesome, a suppository or enema may be given as the patient is placed on the toilet or bedpan to relieve him.

With regard to the patient's physical comfort, the medical supply store can often help you there as well. They stock special pillows, walkers, crutches, hospital beds, gowns — almost anything you need to attend to the patient's needs.

Since the physical care of the elderly infirm requires strength, stamina, and at least some degree of nursing skills, you will want to take advantage of every aid you can find. Older patients' incontinence often leaves a home nurse baffled. For instance, if a woman must always wear a catheter, a visiting nurse will instruct you on its use. Cleanliness is a primary goal since infections can be extremely taxing on an older system. Not only must the bag be emptied at regular intervals, but the catheter itself must be removed and the area cleaned thoroughly. One patient swears that a glass of cranberry juice every day keeps her bladder free from infection.

Men patients have a similar problem inasmuch as the penis is sometimes subjected to the urine in the catheter. Again, this area must be cleansed daily with great care, probably at the same time as the catheter is changed.

Medical supply stores also carry a canvas lift to help in transferring patients from bed to chair or into the bathtub. Formerly home nurses were trained in the techniques of bathing bedridden patients with a sponge bath. Now the relatively inexpensive lift makes it possible for all but the very weak to have a warm tub bath — often therapeutic in itself. Small benches, manufactured expressly for the purpose of supporting frail patients in the bathtub, are also available since the elderly often find it difficult to sit flat in a tub.

Modesty of the patient in bathing, or dressing and undressing, should be considered. Simply because old people are failing does not mean that they have lost all of their need for personal privacy. Large towels or bathing sheets can be draped in such a way as to protect them when they are naked, and doors should always be closed when the patient is in a state of undress.

Shampoos can be simplified so that all but the critically ill can enjoy the feeling of clean hair and scalp. If a patient is mobile, or in a wheelchair, he can be moved to a sink where he can rest his head backward over the edge and have his hair shampooed. Those in bed can take advantage of dry shampoo, which, although it may be a poor substitute for suds and conditioner, is still refreshing to a patient with oily hair.

Toenails are often a problem with the elderly. As we grow older, nails sometimes thicken to the point where it is almost impossible to cut them. Some nursing homes have a standing appointment with a podiatrist to cut patients' toenails, simply because he has the tools to do the job, and the skill to avoid infection which a less well-trained person might initiate. Poor circulation in the extremities leads readily to infection if the skin is penetrated, or if a hangnail results.

Care of the mouth in the elderly is also important. Besides making them feel fresher, cleaning the teeth or dentures and letting them rinse with a nice-tasting mouthwash retards dental problems. Teeth and gums are often the site of infection but this can usually be avoided by scrupulous care.

One of the biggest problems in the elderly who are bedridden is bedsores. The patient's skin should be examined during the course of each bath for red spots which indicate that he is lying or sitting too long on one area. These red areas should be cleaned thoroughly, then powdered and massaged gently, but the main prevention of further sores is to change the patient's position. Donuts or lambskins—again available at medical supply stores—bathing, and massage are the most reliable preventative measures and because, once developed, open and running, these sores are slow to heal, prevention is the wisest course.

Sometimes aged parents complain about minor aches and pains, and well-meaning caretakers are reluctant to take the responsibility for judging the severity of the discomfort. Obviously one can't telephone the doctor about every twinge an aging body might feel. One geriatrician advises that a simple aspirin, or its substitute, a gentle massage, a heating pad, or a warm bath may comfort the patient and decrease the muscle cramps he may feel from sitting or lying too long in one position. If none of these home remedies seem to relieve the patient's discomfort, then it is time to call the doctor. Don't listen at length to symptoms, however, for older bodies are susceptible to all kinds of minor discomforts and exaggerated symptoms which make for good conversation, and the elderly patient may gain attention by complaining.

Other symptoms common in old age are irregular heart-beat, giddiness, belching, a dry mouth, and shortness of breath. These may be insignificant—except to the patient!—and the caretaker would be wise to treat them calmly with the afore-mentioned home remedies before calling in a doctor. If the patient is not relieved, of course, then the doctor should be called.

Edema, swelling or puffiness of the extremities, is also noticable in the aged from time to time. Elevation of the affected limb, or arm, and a warm bath should help to reduce the swelling. Edema is usually due to a cramped position or lack of movement, but since it can also be a manifestation of a more serious illness, the caretaker should observe if the swelling is reduced by these simple treatments. If not, then—again—it is time to call in the doctor.

My husband's hands swelled to twice their size, it seemed, once he was admitted to the nursing home. I inquired about it and learned that, because he paced the halls all day long with his hands hanging at his side, his fingers became enlarged. The purchase of a small nerf ball solved the problem. When I went to visit him, I pulled out the ball and we took turns squeezing it. His hands soon returned to normal.

Cautious Use of Drugs

Included in the care of the elderly is a significant increase in the use of drugs. Most pharmacists admit that the elderly are among those who use the most drugs, and although most of these are prescription drugs, administered under a doctor's written order rather than over-the-counter non-prescription drugs, there is still a grave danger in their use, and certainly in combinations of drugs used by the elderly. Many drugs contraindicate each other, particularly in the older body, and the perceptive caretaker and physician should be wary of unusual symptoms resulting after the use of certain medications. The following quotation is helpful:

DRUGS AND THE ELDERLY (over 60 years of age)

"Advancing age brings changes in body structure and function that may alter significantly the action of drugs. An impaired digestive system may interfere with drug absorption. Reduced capacity of the liver and kidneys to metabolize and eliminate drugs may result in the accumulation of drugs in the body to toxic levels. By impairing the body's ability to maintain a 'steady state' (homeostasis), the aging process may increase the sensitivity of many tissues to the actions of drugs, thereby altering greatly the responsiveness of the nervous and circulatory systems to standard drug doses. If aging should cause deterioration of understanding, memory, vision, or physical coordination, people with such impairments may not always use drugs safely and effectively.

"Adverse reactions to drugs occur three times more frequently in the older population. An unwanted drug response can render a functioning and independent older person, whose health and reserves are at marginal levels, confused, incompetent, or helpless. For these reasons, drug treatment in the elderly must always be accompanied by the most careful consideration of the individual's health and tolerances, the selection of drugs and dosage schedules, and the possible need for assistance in treatment routines."[26]

Guidelines for the use of drugs by the elderly are listed as follows:

- Be certain that drug treatment is necessary. Many health problems of the elderly can be managed without the use of drugs.
- Avoid if possible the use of many drugs at one time. It is advisable to use not more than three drugs concurrently.
- Dosage schedules should be as uncomplicated as possible. When feasible, a single daily dose of each drug is preferable.
- In order to establish individual tolerance, treatment with most drugs is usually best begun by using smaller

than standard doses. Maintenance doses should also be
determined carefully. A maintenance dose is often
smaller for persons over 60 than for younger persons.
•Avoid large tablets and capsules if other dosage forms
are available. Liquid preparations are easier for the
elderly or debilitated to swallow.
•Have all drug containers labeled with the drug name
and directions for use in large, easy-to-read letters.
•Ask the pharmacist to package drugs in easy-to-open
containers. Avoid "child-proof" caps and stoppers.
•Do not take any drug in the dark. Identify each dose of
medicine carefully in adequate light to be certain you
are taking the drug intended.
•To avoid taking the wrong drug or an extra dose, do not
keep drugs on a bedside table. Drugs for emergency
use, such as nitroglycerin, are an exception. It is advisable
to have only one such drug at the bedside for use during
the night.
•Drug use by older persons may require supervision. Observe drug effects continuously to ensure safe and effective use.[27]

The principle of educating the patient to recognize and
accept his rightful share of responsibility in the use of drugs
has not been applied to drug therapy in general, and certainly
not to the geriatric patient who may be incapable of discern-
ing differences in his own reactions, or levels of response, to
medications. Therefore, the caretaker's responsibility must
be intensified in this direction.

Although this chapter has barely touched the subject of
learning to care for the physical needs of the elderly, the
conscientious caretaker may consult one of several splendid
books on home nursing (some of which are named in the
bibliography at the end of this handbook) to learn more
techniques for keeping a loved one happier and more healthy
in his declining years.

_____CHAPTER 4

SATISFYING OTHER NEEDS

"There is tragedy in the physical transformation of the human body and the mind has to live with this transformation, although it is unchanged except for the social and apparent changes in its vehicle."[28]

Difficult as it may be to believe, old people feel much the same as they did when they were young—not in their physical make up, of course, but in their minds, their personalities, their essential selves. The story of a frail literary personage fortifies this theory. Oliver Wendell Holmes outlasted all of his contemporaries. Thin to the point of emaciation and as weak as a leaf in a gale, his mind was still alert and working. One of his acquaintances, without taking much thought, asked him one day, "How are you, Judge Holmes?" His answer is legendary.

"I myself, sir, am fine. This house I live in is sadly in need of repairs, but I myself am fine!"

Oldsters as People

Sometimes we forget that old people are still people with distinct needs, desires, and goals. If we are to relate to them, we must consider their total selves as we plan for their future. Too easily they are written off as *having lived*, not as *living*. Caretakers are often "tempted to treat their parents as children; and they are not children"[29] although their physical needs may be similar. When caring for our elderly, we must remember to recognize our parents' wishes, our own filial maturity and the closeness, or lack of closeness, we have established through the years.

One aging lady stated: "I have four children, yet if I thought I would be pressed to live with either of my sons, I would rather leave this earth prematurely, for they have shown little understanding of my personal problems or desires even as I have lived in good health. Surely we would have little in common if I should become dependent. In such a case I fear that I would feel myself to be a tremendous burden, an interloper in my old age, just as I have seemed to them in my productive years.

"My daughters, on the other hand, would both welcome me into their homes, and there I would feel like an integral part of the family, even though there might be times when we would have to hold a council to keep from imposing on each other, the generations holding differing views as they do. After a dialogue, we could come to some conclusions, which at the present my sons and I could never reach, simply because we do not communicate well."

Most old people want continued concern and affection, with contacts to assure them that their children can be depended on, but, still, they want to remain independent as long as possible.

One elderly woman, living alone in a senior citizen subsidized apartment complex a nation apart from her only daughter, enjoys having her own little apartment and her freedom. In the past year her nearest sister, who lives in the same building, has become infirm, with the result that Mary, let's call her, has run her legs off as an unpaid private nurse. A typical week found her cooking all of her sister's meals, doing her laundry, changing her bed, shopping for all of her groceries—and paying for most of them—and trotting down to her sister's apartment about twenty times a day. Incidentally, Mary, at 83, is not in much better health than her sister who is only one year older!

When Mary's daughter came to visit, she quickly sized up the situation. She tried to regulate her aunt's medicine and stabilize her condition so that Mary wouldn't wear herself out with nursing duties. She even offered to be on call for her aunt at any time of the day or night. The aunt never called her—nor did she cooperate with her niece's efforts to help. It seemed she wanted only the complete attention of her sister.

Before the end of the daughter's visit, she knew something had to be done. Her mother was exhausted, sick, and not far from a complete physical collapse herself. Taking her mother by the shoulders she said, "Mother, I care about you. I am not going to let you kill yourself taking care of someone who should be in a nursing home. Unless you make some other arrangements, and soon, I am coming back to pack you up and take you home with me." The mother looked stricken. She would be states away from all her friends, her usual activities, the cemetery where her husband was buried. Seeing her concern, the daughter continued. "Now, Mother, I think you're happy here, and I would like to see you continue to live in your own little place and be independent as long as you can. I'll do everything to insure that, but you cannot continue as you are. I am serious about this. I will not let you kill yourself."

Apparently that was the lecture that Mary needed. That same day she called her sister's doctor who promptly made a house call and arranged to admit the older woman into the hospital, from which, several weeks later, she was taken to a nursing home.

Freed from almost impossible burdens, Mary has bounced back and is starting to enjoy life once more, though she continues to visit her sister at the nursing home.

Loss of Control

Sometimes a daughter or son can best serve their parents by fortifying their position. In Mary's case, she knew she was overdoing, but out of misplaced sibling loyalty, she would have continued to burden herself. Her daughter's no-nonsense declaration gave her the out she needed.

Elderly parents know they are losing control over their lives; they need a helping hand to continue normal functions. The adult child must acquire the capacity to be depended upon. "Family communication and closeness are essential for living out one's years in dignity and peace."[30] Phone calls, visiting, and just plain caring can carry an elderly parent over many a rough hump. "Everywhere the human cycle begins with the dependency of the young on those who are older, and usually ends with the dependency of the very old on those who are younger."[31]

Imagine yourself with half of your eyesight lost, all of your teeth, a quarter of your hearing, and half of your ability to move quickly, becoming a burden to your children, perhaps by having to move into their home, or by being dependent upon them for support. You've given up your business because of old age, poor health, or both, so you must learn a new way of life. You're also in pain some of the time and your digestive system is shot—probably because your daughter-in-law doesn't know how to cook like your wife. And the kids are too noisy . . . and disrespectful to boot. No wonder you feel so miserable. There's no place for you, not here, not anywhere in the whole world.

How would you feel under these circumstances? Old age is a new experience, undergone by people who have learned another way of life and have been fairly well satisfied with it. Now, when they are least able to adjust, they are faced with what seems like insurmountable problems . . . and no one cares or understands. They feel as if they are treated like the furniture, with no control over their surroundings. So they have temper tantrums, they pout, they frequently show impatience, and they often ask for sympathy for real or imagined physical ailments.

Knowing how they feel, the perceptive caretaker gives them the attention they need (and want) but she does not hover nor encourage excessive complaints. With kind but firm discipline, in an unemotional manner, the caretaker tries to maintain a routine for the oldster similar to the one he was accustomed to in his old home. He should not be exposed to violence, such as children's quarrels, nor even to too much action of a violent nature on TV because it will upset him. He should be encouraged to dress himself, to get out and around as much as he can, and to pursue his own interests and friends. When he is not too steady on his feet, perhaps someone in the family can see to it that he gets out to visit with others of his own age group. Often oldsters enjoy talking about their common symptoms, their obsession with catching cold, faulty bowel movements, surgical experiences, their latest medicines or physicians, etc. They need their own generation to commiserate with, to communicate with, to exchange feelings with.

Religious Activity

Religion can play a large part in an aging person's life. If he has been religious in his earlier years, surely he'll want to continue with the same activities as before if he can without undue discomfort. But even if faith has not been an active part of his younger years, he may find great comfort in church attendance. Many church organizations realize the needs of older members. They furnish them with opportunities, not only for worship, but also for discussions, book reviews, handwork, or women's organizations, games, and—frequently—lunches.

The elderly view life in a more dramatic way than younger people. Questions occur to them about the meaning of life. Why am I living? Why can't I die? Will I see my wife beyond the grave? Indeed, is there life beyond the grave? What is the meaning of life? All of these questions, and more, take on new meaning as one anticipates his own death. The aged are more philosophical about these urgent questions. They even talk about death, a subject generally avoided in polite company. Such talk should be given the respect it deserves. If you find it difficult to discuss such issues, you might encourage a visit by the older person's pastor, or another member of his congregation. The patient may wish to talk also about his sins, or shortcomings (a sort of last-minute repentance), and trained personnel are knowledgeable about how to accept such confessions. In some churches last rites are an important ritual, and if the patient feels this way, by all means respect his requests.

Normal Needs

But what if the parent is well enough to consider his life on another level, like remarriage for instance? Sometimes two older people marry because they can manage to live more cheaply together than apart. In this instance, children should spare their parent the added trauma of their disapproval. Give them your blessing, go to the wedding, and invite them over to dinner frequently. You may find that "Dad" will take on added vigor and enthusiasm with a new bride. At any rate, it is his life and his decision, and you must make the best of it.

Even if "Dad" is not matrimonially oriented, he needs some changes from time to time. See that he goes out to dinner, to community programs, to see the children perform at school—whatever he enjoys. If he is inclined to want to stay at home bring in other people he might have something in common with, or at least take him outdoors for part of the day when the weather is nice. A change in scenery is usually refreshing even if he is well enough to move only from room to room.

Take advantage of community facilities such as talking books for the visually impaired . . . or the public library if the patient's eyes are still good enough to make reading enjoyable. *Reader's Digest* publishes a large-print issue every month, and many older readers enjoy keeping up-to-date with a magazine they have read all their lives.

Communities frequently sponsor free transportation, or charge small fees for transportation, that will carry handicapped or older citizens to places of interest. Many of the vehicles are equipped with lifts for wheelchairs. Going on a "trip" usually motivates the patient to "dress up" in his best attire, since he'll be seeing other people, probably at their best, too. In fact, it's a good idea to motivate dressing up from time to time because grooming plays a large part in how we feel about ourselves. A new permanent or dress may relieve depression for weeks. Besides, while "Grandma" is getting a permanent, the caretaker has a little free time to do something for herself—also important in the growing relationship between two generations.

Regular Breaks for Caretakers

And don't overlook the needs of the caretaker. A patient can sense resentment if a caretaker has been on duty for too long. Everyone in this position should be relieved on a regular basis by a paid substitute or a member of the family. Too often the bulk of the responsibility falls on one member, burdening him to such an extent that the doctor ends up with two patients. No one can work a 24-hour-a-day shift for long without crumbling either emotionally or physically, or both. Families must share in the obligations. If they won't, the caretaker should see to it that they contribute in some other way, like paying for the sitter, for instance, or medical equipment needed by the patient. That's the least they can do if they don't want to be bothered with "Dad."

Tragedies of Old Age

But whoever cares for the older member of the family, someone must, or else we may hear the isolated, lonely old man or woman offer this classic prayer:

Now I lay me down to sleep.
I pray the Lord my soul will keep.
If I should die before I wake,
Who the hell would care?

Statistics bear out the fact that 5 million Americans are destined to die alone and unattended, sometimes unnoticed for days or even weeks. What a tragedy. Everyone should have the right to die with his loved ones gathered around him. "There is no single feature of the human situation that produces more universal loss and suffering, both physical and mental, than the process of aging."[32]

Some way must be found to attend to these aging citizens, to let them know they are loved and cared for, to give them security in their dotage. It seems reasonable to assume that the major responsibility should rest on the family. The time may come when the patient must be turned over to professionals, but until that time he should have every right to feel himself an integral part of a family unit in a home where he is loved and respected for himself; not for what he has become or for what his children will inherit when he finally dies.

The suicide rate for those over 65 is 20 percent higher than the national average for all groups. Old people, finding themselves with empty lives and empty days, universally find themselves depressed because they seem to be ignored by a society that has no use for them. Everyone needs at least a modicum of attention, and if the elderly are listened to with respect and shown natural signs of affection, they can be drawn back into the land of the living.

When one old man was finally admitted into a rest home, his wife visited every day for weeks. She wasn't well herself. She walked with a cane and seemed paper-thin. Nevertheless, she visited her husband who hardly knew she was there. Finally the attendants tried to persuade her to miss a day or two and stay home to rest. She would have nothing to do with their suggestions. She didn't want anyone else to take her place in her husband's life, and she told them so in no uncertain terms.

Everyone is not so fortunate as to have a devoted mate survive him. Many old people find themselves entirely alone in the world. Their closest relatives have preceeded them in death, and cousins, aunts, etc., lost track of them through busy lives which seldom intersected.

To Mrs. R. in Los Angeles, to be old means "being so lonely I could die." An elderly widow, she lives in a crowded apartment near a freeway with no one to give her the time of day. In a letter to the *Los Angeles Times* she wrote:

"I see no human beings. My phone never rings. I feel sure the world has ended. I'm the only one (left) on earth. How else can I feel? The people here won't talk to you. They say, 'Pay your rent and go back to your room.' I'm so lonely, very, very much. I don't know what to do. . . ."

She enclosed with her letter six stamps and a dollar bill, and asked for someone to call her or write to her. Pathetic.

The Need to be Needed

Few of us realize it, but older citizens can contribute uniquely to society, as proved by the Foster Grandparent program and any number of other organizations formed to keep America's oldsters busy, and to help children and teenagers as well. Many men and women over 65 act as tutors in schools where the teacher is overworked or where there is a problem with underachievement, learning disabilities or discipline. Some of these "jobs" pay a small salary to the volunteer which helps him out at the end of the month when Social Security funds have been spent.

Many other seniors work as volunteers in their churches, civic organizations, or for their favorite political party. Whatever they choose to do, the activity keeps them from feeling left out. They make a distinct contribution to the world. Therefore, they feel a part of it. And they have something to talk about besides their aches and pains. As one old gentleman says, "I've never been so busy in my life. It's a good thing I retired, or I wouldn't have time to go to work."

New research undermines the old notion that mental decline is a natural, inevitable feature of old age. The way to keep mentally alert is to stay active, interested, and challenged by life. Besides acting as Foster Grandparents, older citizens can participate in such activities as Green Thumb, as aides for the National Association of Retired Persons and the Service Corps of Retired Executives, and in such organizations as Senior Committee Service Projects, the Bureau of Census Interviews, Vista, the Peace Corps, Retired Citizen Senior Volunteer Program, and the National Center for Volunteer Action. They may also volunteer at local hospitals or sell savings bonds. The list is lengthy, but oldsters who want to work on a volunteer basis can do so.

Everyone wants to feel useful. Even patients in rest homes. My husband's faithful friend, Ortho, followed him around like a loyal watchdog. One day when I came to visit, I noticed that Frank's trousers were slipping down his hips. His belt was nowhere in sight. More as a topic of conversation than anything else, I asked Ortho, "Frank isn't wearing his belt. Do you have any idea where it might be?" Ortho had retained more power of communication than Frank and he answered with assurance, "Yes, I have it right here in my pocket." "Good," I responded. "Let's put it on him, shall we?"

"No problem," he replied, extending his clenched fist, fingers down, toward me. I reached out for the proferred belt and felt something cold and hard hit my palm—Ortho's false teeth!

Neither of the men noticed anything amiss, but I graciously returned the dentures and thanked Ortho, saying that he had better use for them than Frank. Later we found the missing belt, curled up in Ortho's false teeth cup. I was deeply touched by this sweet old man's efforts to be helpful. Of course, he knew where the belt was. He wanted part of the action, as we all do.

Interdependence

The elderly make up 10 percent of the total population. That's almost 20 million people—too many to declare obsolete. And, contrary to popular opinion, only 7 percent live in institutions. Thirty percent live alone or with non-relatives, and the remaining 63 percent still live with their spouses or with their children. Many of these 63 percent could be given small jobs to lighten the load of working parents, perhaps, with Granddad trimming the hedge and Grandmother sorting the socks . . . or doing some other chores which wouldn't be too arduous for the old folks but helpful to the family.

Elaine Brody of the Philadelphia Geriatric Center says: "The cultural value which emphasizes independence as the desired goal often obscures the psychological truth that interdependence is normal and healthy throughout the life cycle. Total separation and total dependence are as pathological as over-involvement and over-dependence."[33] In other words, there's room for the old folks in your life. Move over and make room for them.

If you make an older person's life important, he will live a happier life . . . and probably longer, too. In time the human life span may extend to 100 years—or even 110—and life expectancy may be extended even further.

Because senescence is built into the human machine, we shouldn't expect it to fail at 65 years of age. Children can be taught patience, sacrifice, compassion, consideration, and loving kindness if they are encouraged to share in the care of their grandparents, not write them off as soon as they seem to show signs of aging. The continuity formed between the two or three generations by a graceful merging can be a lifeline for all of them. For, if there is anything the old have to teach the young, it is serenity, and we all need that. "In a changing world the helpless aged as well as the helpless young give us a sense of responsibility and a feeling of continuity."[34]

In our modern lives and social interaction the separation between the generations is not made by either the aged or the young, but, rather, by those in the middle who feel, somehow, that if the old are hidden their dreadful condition will not pass on to them. They try to make the aged invisible because old age, to them, is a threat to society; that if the old could gradually disappear, without causing worry or discomfort, everyone would be happier.

Eyes are averted, explanations made, and Grandpa's standards or forgetfulness are rejected because he is "old." How much more healthy is a proud acceptance of the old folks as real people who have contributed to society and made us what we are. Make them feel your gratitude and you will satisfy their deepest needs.

"Honor thy father and thy mother:
that thy days may be long upon the land
which the Lord thy God giveth thee."
                    Exodus 20:12

_____CHAPTER 5

Finances and Housing

An old saying implies that aging is a matter of money, genetics, and luck. There's not much to be done about the last two, but money seems to be the variable that must be controlled if the elderly are to look forward to security in their declining years. "Freedom from money cares is perhaps the best medicine an old person can have."[35]

When oldsters must worry about finances as well as failing health, housing problems, and relationships that aren't as satisfying as they would like, their lives become infinitely more troubled. Not only does their physical health decline, but they grow bitter and often feel neglected—for good reason. With a steady income they feel the comfort of being cared for, especially if money is given to them regularly, and gladly, by their children. Even if a parent lives with a grown child who furnishes everything he needs for sustenance, the older person needs money of his own so that he can feel free to purchase small comforts.

From the minds of such professionals as a doctor, an attorney, and a mortician, I have learned that grown children are often like vultures, hardly waiting until the "old folks" die to start picking at the carcass of their meager possessions, scraps of property, and personal items. And money that may be left after the parents are taken care of is fought over like African diamonds. Sometimes this battle starts even before the parents die when they are helpless and in great need of family support.

Liquidate Holdings

It seems reasonable that any property, or stocks and bonds, should be liquidated to provide for elderly parents, but selfish children often do not see it that way. They prefer to keep their parents in dire straits rather than to forfeit their own future inheritance. But even life insurance should be cashed in if the parents have needs that cannot be met in other ways. After all, they provided for the children when they were growing up. Now it is their turn to be aided and supported.

Many older children have parents with no financial problems, but the odds against this are increasing as prices escalate and people live longer to become more fragile and in need of more care.[36] For the ten-year period from 1972 to 1982, all items in the Consumer Price Index rose 131 percent, medical services 158 percent, food 131 percent, gas/electricity 227 percent (national figure) and transportation 143 percent.[37] If you are elderly, and alive, in 1985, you know how much money it takes to live—far more than it did even two years ago and far more than you have. Money is the elderly citizen's greatest problem.

As the older population expands, this problem will intensify. Dr. Harold Sheppard, economist with the American Institute of Research, says that the proportion of oldsters is growing at a dazzling rate. In 1960, according to his figures, there were thirty-four 80-year-olds for every person between 60 and 65 in this country. In 1970, there were forty-six. By 1990 he estimates that there will be sixty-three; and by the year 2000, there will be a staggering number of 80-year-olds— eighty for every one hundred people between 60 and 65 years of age.[38]

Confronted with figures like this, we can see that financial burdens will increase proportionally. It is even suggested that, by the year 2020, four generations living under the same roof will not be unusual. Nursing homes cannot handle this increase, nor can family or government budgets carry the financial load. Families may be forced to support their old people, whether they think they can or not.

Changing Patterns

Yet the trends in sociological groupings oppose this. Some years ago most families were self-employed on farms, or in small businesses, and the more children they had the more help they recruited to work the family enterprise. People retired gradually, if at all. The tendency today is away from rural living and self-employment. Seven out of ten workers retire at 65 with only a small pension and Social Security to rely on for a living. Their families are usually scattered and living in small apartments, or homes, where old folks are not welcome. Few families accrue enough savings to provide separate housing for their aged parents since their weekly salary often barely covers the needs of their immediate family. There is simply no money — no room — for Grandpa!

Care of an aging parent generally falls on an unmarried child, or the oldest daughter, or the wife of the oldest son. Too often, this person, or family, carries the entire burden of support. Ideally, all children should share in the responsibility although outside sources may be sought for supplementary income and help. The main support should come from the children of the senior member of the family or, perhaps, from other close relatives.

Sharing the Care

Realistically, however, one family or child usually gets the brunt of the burden. Yet if a family council is held to determine what each child can offer, a compromise plan can sometimes be worked out. If the family cannot agree on their own, perhaps a counselor should be called in, preferably one with experience in dealing with the aged and their problems. Admittedly, these are hard to find. Consult a telephone directory for Community Health Centers or Family and Child Service Agencies. Some churches and synagogues offer similar services.

At any rate, after you've found a counselor, consider the factors in discussing how to support "Dad": the older person's wishes, the degree of filial maturity in each child, the income of each, and the amount of closeness that each child

has with his parent. Usually the offspring will be against putting Dad into a nursing home; each one, in fact, may offer to
take the old man into his own home. This seldom works,
however, and Dad may be pushed from pillar to post like a
pendulum until the poor old fellow is so confused he'd be
better off in a nursing home. At least he'd have a chance to
learn the location of the light switches and the bathroom.

Most offers to care for Dad are merely manifestations
of guilt. Ask the children, instead, for money to enable Dad
to live in his own home, and you'll see how sincere are their
offers to help. This is one of the reasons a professional counselor should help in making decisions. Children are too fraught
with feelings of guilt and "duty" to make logical, rational
decisions based on facts.

The family council should be held well in advance of
the crisis, and after considering a parent's wishes, each child
should commit to do his best; sending a little money, perhaps;
or making time for regular visits, depending on their resources.
A person with limited capacity already has enough guilt.
Merely accept whatever he is able to contribute, but make
certain it is a regular and dependable contribution.

One reason for selecting a family counselor is that professionals are usually acquainted with alternatives available
in the community. If a child is chosen to care for the elderly
parent simply because she is only a housewife, or — in other
words — unemployed, this is hardly a suitable recommendation. Perhaps her health is poor. In this case she would not
have the stamina needed to care for an infirm or helpless
patient. The family council should consider the following:

- Will the care of the patient put too great a demand on
  the caretaker?
- Does the potential caretaker have the ability to care for
  the patient?
- Can you accept the fact that she can't handle it and
  seek another solution?
- Have you considered the problems of the entire family,
  not just the caretaker or the aged person?

Children, after all, cannot kill themselves caring for their
aged parents. Many try to do just that when they are forced

by other siblings to assume the full responsibility of care. If the family council meets, it can come to some terms before the situation is critical when everyone can be a part of the planning, as well as the solution, without undue emotional pressures.

Alternate Solutions

Listen to the professional when he lists possibilities for alternative action. If the older family member is able to stay in his own home, with a little help, consider these options:

- •A housekeeper or a health aide who comes in as needed.
- •Homemakers, Inc., who work by the hour, again as needed.
- •Visiting Nurse Association when skilled nursing is needed on a part-time basis.
- •Meals on Wheels, which furnishes a hot meal daily five days a week for a small fee or food stamps. (This organization even caters to those who require special diets.)
- •Senior Centers which serve hot lunches and supply older citizens with opportunities for companionship with others in their own age group; hobbies, crafts, entertainment, etc., either free or for a small fee.
- •Day Care, usually supplied by Senior Centers, which provide supervision for oldsters unable to be left alone while others in the family are away from home. Often the charge is based on a sliding scale, according to income. The oldster goes to his own home each night.

Even if the elderly citizen cannot remain in his own home, other options are possible. He may be able to work a part-time job which will offer him a little spending money as well as making him feel like a contributing member of society. In addition, a job gives him somewhere to go each day for a few hours and might make living with a relative more pleasant for everyone concerned.

In some communities, different forms of communal living are available. In one city, a church sponsored the erection of a large, three-bedroom apartment house especially for older renters. These tenants are able to move in their own possessions like a bedroom set, a favorite rocker, etc. As a result, they feel

more at home. Three or more seniors live together. They help
one another, and they hire help for whatever chores they cannot handle themselves. They prove to be surprisingly self-
sufficient. What one can't do, another usually can . . . and does.
Receiving help from another oldster is not nearly as demean-
ing as being totally dependent, for instance, on a son.

Live-in help is another option. Although help is difficult to
find in many cities, if the magic combination between helper
and helpee can be worked out this often leads to a life-long
association. Live-in help is often too expensive, however, because
housekeepers are not as willing now to work for board and
room, as they once were.

Other possibilities include apartment complexes or retirement villages where, again, the residents look after each other.
Some organizations have a telephone committee which calls
all tenants at least once a day, usually just before bedtime, to
see if they are all right. These apartments may be subsidized by
organizations such as churches or civic groups so that the rent is
based on income, and, therefore, more affordable for most
seniors. The big plus in accommodations like these is the close
companionship that develops among residents. They are not
alone. They have each other, regardless of negligent children or
thoughtless friends.

Custodial Care

Probably the last option a family wishes to consider is a
rest or nursing home, yet often this facility may provide the care
the patient needs. No one should feel the road to a nursing
home is a one-way street; that they go there simply to die. Many
homes release patients after they recouperate from accidents or
strokes, for instance, and patients formerly unable to care for
themselves return to normal living patterns. Some homes take
patients on a part-time basis, something like Day Centers, except
that they care for the patient through the week while their families take a vacation "Dad" wouldn't enjoy, for instance, or
merely to get a well-deserved break. Some nursing-home residents spend days, or even weekends with their families, or go
out to lunch or dinner, or to a show. As long as they are able to

do this, their families should make such contacts with the outer world possible.

One son, thinking of himself as dutiful, mourned the fact that his father had been admitted to a nursing home. He couldn't wait to take his dad out for a ride, or back to his home to see all the grandchildren. It was several weeks before the staff felt the elderly man was up to an excursion, but finally they gave their permission and the son picked up his dad for the day. In an hour he was back with tears in his eyes. He let the old man off at the gate, not even walking into the hall with him. Later the attendants learned that the old man was "restless," that the son didn't know what to do with him so he brought him right back — without dinner, without the planned visit with his family.

Unfortunately, children don't always know what is best for their aging parents. Rest home administrators and staff should always be consulted before children make plans since they usually know what is best for the patient.

But simply because your parent is in a custodial facility does not mean you should avoid him. Many older patients enjoy card games, visits, gifts, or phone calls from their loved ones. Even though they may not be as alert as the children would wish them to be they usually know that someone has cared enough to come to see them. Some of them brag for days afterwards that their "boy" came to visit. Snapshots and other mementoes of former family ties are valued treasures in nursing homes.

"Placement in a nursing home is usually less socially acceptable solution to a problem than remaining in one's own home."[39] And a further comment: "But the longer people live, the greater is the likelihood that they will develop disabling conditions requiring protective or skilled care."[40] And, "Far from being a waiting room for death, nursing homes can represent, for some, a new and meaningful phase in their life."[41]

A directory of acceptable nursing homes is published by the American Association of Homes for the Aging. Family members will find this source a great help in searching out the right facility for their parent.

The decision must often be based on money available for the patient's care. Medicare and Medicaid have built-in limitations which sometimes preclude admission. Some will not admit a patient unless Medicare will pay for his care from the beginning; others require private financing for the first month to determine the patient's eligibility for Medicare or Medicaid. Many families cannot raise the $1400 or more that a private nursing home charges each month—not even for one month.

When I realized that my husband's mental condition was rapidly deteriorating, I made a serious investigation of rest-home facilities within a 150-mile radius of our home. Many had long waiting lists, and most administrators I talked to explained that the full cost would have to be paid in advance—from $1200 to $1400 per month—until my husband's needs could be assessed and his eligibility for Medicaid determined.

My investigation was discouraging, to say the least. We were not monied people although we had always taken pride in the fact that we paid our own bills. There was hardly $1200 in our bank account to admit him, much less pay for a prolonged stay month after month. We simply did not have that kind of income, and we weren't certain he would be eligible for Medicaid because his situation was purely custodial. In his case, there was no hope for rehabilitation.

At about this time I heard about the ruggedly independent man who had placed his critically ill wife in a nursing home after an initial stay in a hospital. The first month he paid cash for her care. The second month he investigated Medicaid only to learn that he owned too much property to qualify. He continued to pay for her care until one year had passed. Surprisingly, her condition remained stable but she was not well enough to return home. And so it went, month after month, as he sold property or borrowed on it to take care of medical bills. The second year she qualified. He had spent his whole life's savings and reduced his properties down to one small home where he lived . . . and it was mortgaged.

In desperation, I decided to investigate one more home—a small private facility outside of town where a student of mine was employed. What a difference. This remodeled home in a residential area housed only sixteen patients, mostly men. The head nurse told me that, although they were licensed for twenty-eight, they would never have more than twenty. The administrator wanted to retain the homey atmosphere and personal relationship each patient enjoyed.

I stood there chatting with the head nurse who was well-informed and friendly. One of the nearby patients, an elderly man who had lost the benefit of speech, sat crookedly in a wheelchair demanding attention. His words resembled the garbled communication of a severely retarded person.

The nurse excused herself and put her arm around the old man's bony shoulders.

"Willie, dear, I know you need attention, but this lady's husband is sick, too, and she needs to talk to me. Could you wait just a minute, then I'll take care of you." The love, the respect in her voice, and her body language won me over more than anything she might have told me. A few months later Frank was admitted. Since that time I have been a regular visitor. Never have I heard a patient spoken to by any of the attendants with less than love and consideration.

Small homes have their advantages. Each person is treated like an individual, staff members are easily monitored, everyone feels like "family," and the cost of care was about half the cost of others I had investigated. Also, this home has a less institutionalized atmosphere. The staff seems happy and contented with their positions. I have never regretted admitting him there.

The situation must be quite different in some homes. Sometimes attendants, because they must handle the aging bodies of these old people, begin to treat them as if they were infants—unhearing, uncaring, unable to speak or communicate in any way. Patients are often called "dearie" or "honey" and scolded like naughty children when they soil their beds. "Sometimes patients are treated as inanimate objects, rather than as any kind of human being, adult or infant."[42]

If a parent must be institutionalized, how much better to seek out a facility that treats him with kindness and compassion rather than housing him in a sterile, modern building. A cold, unfeeling attitude by staff members indicates the atmosphere and the general philosophy of the care center. In my case I opted for human warmth.

Helpful Considerations

The following are questions to help you decide which home to choose, and certainly they should be considered. In the end, however, place your loved one where both you and he will be most comfortable.

1. Are there opportunities for socialization? Recreational opportunities?
2. Is there respect for privacy for individuals? For couples?
3. Is there a resident council?
4. Is consideration given to the selection of roommates? Of tablemates?
5. Does the staff and administration welcome criticism and suggestions from relatives?
6. Is there a relatives' auxiliary with machinery for airing grievances, problems, and suggestions?
7. Are residents treated with respect and dignity?
8. Does the staff deliver affectionate treatment along with competent care?

"The ideal atmosphere combines friendliness, warmth, and concern. It permits residents to maintain a sense of personal dignity. It respects privacy, allows individuality, and has room for some degree of freedom. It is not easy to achieve, and even though it may appear spontaneous and undirected, it usually is just the opposite and results from explicit expectations percolating down from the top—from the Board of Directors and administration through the supervisors and professionals."[43]

Behind the Scenes

At seven P.M. in the nursing home the halls are quiet. Only the more active patients are still up. They are gathered around the kitchen serving window like a cluster of bees around a bright flower. It's "smoke time" I see. Those gathered there grab their cigarettes gratefully from the attendant and troop out to the patio where they enjoy their last smoke of the day.

Back in the kitchen someone is preparing Sunday's dinner—turkey and dressing, yams, and a jello salad. Everything must be soft, or easily chewed, because most of the residents have lost their teeth. The attendants discuss Sunday's breakfast which will be bacon and eggs, but a third girl is baking waffles and stacking them in a large pan to be warmed in the oven in the morning. It's only Friday, but preparations are made in advance, in the dark hours when patients are mostly asleep.

One of the patients comes up to chat with me. He's carrying a dog-earred issue of *Popular Mechanics* which he says features an article about war-time use of submarines. The article may be bonafide; the man's discussion is not. He talks about the Russians and the "war"—his war, I decide. He appears to be about forty. He says he was in the Marines but I don't know whether to believe him or not. A minute earlier he had stated that he *used* to be Irish. Now he's a prisoner of war with a shot in his heart.

You have to take all tales with a grain of salt, I decide, because now he's rambling on about getting the Japs out of the trees in the jungle and onto the ground so he can use a submachine gun. At least his theme repeats itself.

The lives of the patients here are intensely fantastic. Utterly convinced that their stories are true, they still change their versions daily, sometimes hourly.

Today my husband seemed to know me, so tonight I returned to his room but at seven P.M. he's sleeping like a baby, tucked into his narrow bed in a four-bed ward where the most seriously handicapped patients are housed except for those who are bedridden.

In the livingroom area two or three men doze in front of the TV, their chins resting on their chests and their grunts startling them into occasional wakefulness. I wonder why they don't just go to bed, but apparently they have the option of choosing their own bedtime. Great, I think. Their options are few enough.

Attendants alternate hours. At night fewer emergencies arise, fewer demands are made on their time and their backs. Yet there are always tasks to be performed—preparation for the next day, changing a restless patient's diaper, persuading another to return to bed, sorting medication.

My husband is in protective custody; yet I feel good about him resting in these capable and kindly hands. Someone watches over him twenty-four hours a day. I couldn't do that. He has skilled nursing care which I cannot provide. He belongs here, I finally decide. I couldn't care for him at home — not like these professionals do. I leave with a deep feeling of gratitude.

"A patient-oriented, professionally guided, intelligently operated nursing home often is the most humane alternative open to many old people."[44] Such a home provides skilled nursing for 24 hours a day, intensive care, supervision and treatment—far more than I could give him at home.

*"The fathers shall not be put to death
for the children, neither shall the
children be put to death for the fathers."*
Deuteronomy 24:16

_____CHAPTER 6

LETTING GO WITHOUT GUILT

After providing as well as you can for your aging loved one, after giving him the personal and medical attention he requires, at the end there is nothing to do but let go. Those who have acted as responsible sons and daughters do not need to feel guilty; those who haven't usually are torn by feelings of guilt. But both groups experience an element of insecurity, a persistent feeling that insists, "You might have done better."

Even as your loved one is dying, you must handle these feelings and cope with them like a mature person, facing the consequences. Recognize, first of all, that your dad, or mother, is going to die. Denial at this point is particularly destructive. Turn this feeling into a determination to make certain he is not one of the 5 million elderly Americans who die alone and unattended. Give him the full measure of attention and kindness due him as your parent, and as a member of the community, and make his last days happy by confirming the love you've had for him all along. No one can ask for more than that, and a parent will find his heart brimming with the thought that he had a devoted offspring to attend him in his last days on earth.

We all fear death, the young as well as the old, but the old have had more time to think about it. Their minds have grown less quick and alert and their bodies less efficient. They've felt the frustration of inadequacy and the torment of being ignored. They have concerned themselves about the trouble they've caused their family members, and sometimes they're less than ideal patients. Their confusion explodes in sarcasm, irritability, and impatience. They sometimes become depressed as well, and this is a difficult period for you. But forgive them while they're still alive. They'll die so much easier if they have the assurance that you understand.

When my husband started to fail noticeably, his powers of communication were seriously hampered. One time he became angry with himself for not being able to explain something to me. Although I didn't always find the patience to cope with his faltering speech, this time I asked simple questions to clarify his message. Finally he got it out and we rejoiced together.

"Thank you," he said quietly.

"What for?" I asked in surprise.

"For understanding," he answered.

Tears welled up in his eyes. I could have kicked myself for all the times I had failed him. The communication between us was so sweet that I wouldn't have missed it for the world. At last I had learned to understand his condition . . . and his frustration.

As people approach death or serious infirmity, they seem to take a hold on life that exceeds their former values. One old man said, "The older I get, the more chained I feel by all this stuff. I don't need it. Maybe I never did. My role required it: I didn't."[45]

This man was rejecting the need to conform, to gather possessions around him, now that his life was drawing to a close. His "stuff" seemed to keep him from being himself.

By all means, if you can, cater to your loved one's wishes in these matters. If he wants to simplify his life, let him. If he expresses a desire to travel to the Carribean, telephone a travel agent. These "whims" are not what they seem. They may stem from long-suppressed desires that crave to be fulfilled before the final hour of life.

A lovely lady, whose husband preceeded her in death, spends all of her time cruising to foreign lands despite the fact that she underwent a quadruple heart by-pass a couple of years ago and her health is extremely precarious. "I don't want to die at home in bed," she states. "What's the sense of that? Dyk and I had a good life and now that he's gone, I want to carry on our tradition of seeing as much of the world as I can. I can always go home if I want to. Right now I want to travel, to experience new things, new sights, new people." Traveling gives this woman new life. It's hard on her children, of course, but should they be the main concern at this point?

In dealing with an oldster in his declining state, lead him if he'll let you but don't force him to accept your ideas. Try not to rub him the wrong way. He has the right to do as he wishes as long as it doesn't harm anyone. And since the quality of his life may be in question, give him free rein to make decisions about how he spends his last days. If you do, life will be easier for both of you.

The paranoia that often accompanies advanced age may send him into irrational tizzies from time to time. "The mailman is a thief!" he'll scream. Or "You're stealing all my money!" Answer calmly, with objectivity, "You're angry, aren't you?" Or "frightened," or whatever fits the situation. Your understanding of his feelings will do more towards soothing troubled waters than any amount of logic. Actually, he's asking for attention. Give him the right kind, loving understanding, not a chewing-out for his improper reasoning ability—he already senses that. Delusions and a retreat from reality are fairly common in older patients, and if you remove your personal feelings from the picture, and think only of his, you will both come out as winners.

"In the last months of his life my father was confined to a hospital where he was given oxygen to stabilize his condition. Formerly his mind had been alert and quick, but after so much oxygen his mind played tricks on him. One time he told me that the hospital attendants had taken him fishing that morning, and he'd caught the biggest 'grouper' of his life. To illustrate, he lifted feeble arms and measured off the mythical catch. I was taken aback. I hardly knew how to react, but I made some positive statement about how thrilled he must have been. We went on talking and in a few minutes, he looked shamefaced. 'I didn't really catch any fish, did I? I can't even get out of bed.'

" 'No, Dad, I guess you didn't,' I agreed, 'but you surely had a good time, didn't you?' His eyes took on a new luster as he responded, 'I really did!' I wouldn't have taken away that delusion of his for anything!"

Accept your patient's condition instead of mourning about it. Heavy mourning prevents a person from acting rationally, and now is the time when you must provide the guiding light for your older loved one. The child must become the father of the man, even though the role might be somewhat uncomfortable. We don't always understand the reasoning of fate but we can learn to accept it. When your parent is dying you must put off the old man and take on the new. Not only is there a new life approaching for the dying; there is also a new life waiting for you.

Dr. Don Gutmann, clinical psychologist, reveals that old people need to die a "good" death. The patient's life must have stood for something, he should feel a sense of integrity at the end, as if he'd not only paid his dues, but hadn't sold out to fads or trends. Everyone has a strong need to stand up and be counted, Dr. Gutmann says. If the dying person feels he has given his life for a worthy cause, "whether that cause be his family, his job, or his God, he can die in peace."[46]

But love, and your parent's feeling of worth, may not be enough to get you through those last days. You must face your feelings in this emotional tug of war. On the one hand, you are relieved that the constant burden of illness is lifting; on the other hand, you are desolate that you will no longer have your mother (or father) on earth. Any unresolved conflicts you've harbored through the years will undoubtedly surface at this time, making the adjustment doubly difficult.

The family merry-go-round that usually accompanies any stressful situation will probably complicate the process. Again, the best insurance against unnecessary feelings of guilt is the assurance that you did your best for your parents while they lived. Take heart in that, and leave the rest to God.

"We live in a culture which does not wish to concern itself with death or aging. The old walk with death as a close companion yet find few people who will recognize that fact . . . facing death is one of the noblest things about old age.

Strength and dignity, maintained in the face of declining abilities, should be a part of the total life experience."[47]

Of course feelings of guilt arise long before the fatal illness or the funeral. "What to do about Dad?" becomes the hue and cry of many middle-aged children and the solution is never simple. Sometimes, however, we make it harder than it needs to be.

"When off-and-on care or supportive care is necessary for one of your parents, someone must be around to give it, but that someone does not have to be you, or your younger sister, or your older brother. Because society has provided such limited assistance to the elderly, they have been forced to turn to their children for lack of anyone else to turn to. Even today when services are becoming available, your mother may have no idea where to look for help outside of her family. You may not know either and feel obligated to take the responsibility for the care yourself.

"Finding someone to share a burden is not buckpassing or shirking, though it may be labeled that by other family members, friends or neighbors, who may tut-tut when they see a stranger coming in every day to take care of old Mrs. Grenville or an outsider taking Mr. Packer to have his leg brace adjusted. They may enjoy gossiping about Mrs. Grenville's 'unfeeling' daughter or Mr. Packer's 'no-good' son. Meanwhile Mrs. Grenville may be quite content that she has someone to take good care of her, and Mr. Packer may be relieved that his brace can be adjusted regularly without bothering his busy son.

"Both old people may prefer to have their children around when there are fewer chores to do and more time for them to talk and enjoy each other. Modern sons and daughters, so accustomed to feeling guilty about their parents, may overestimate their own roles in their parents' lives. Studies suggest that the older generation, even when it has close ties with their children, sometimes prefers a measure of separation. Why else do so many choose, as one report shows, houses or apartments in retirement villages with no extra bedrooms? This choice may be made not only because of cost or convenience but also to prevent lengthy visits from children and grandchildren."[48]

When competent care is impossible to find or a home is not suitable for old folks, another solution must be found without harboring feelings of guilt. And so it is with nursing facilities. When the time comes that Mother must be admitted to custodial care, find the best home you can for the money you can afford, and place her in it for her own welfare. She may protest at first, but with the passage of time she will probably prefer to stay where there are others with handicaps similar to her own. She may feel more functional, and surely less of a burden than if she were "imposing" on her children, particularly if her savings or pension is large enough to cover her expenses. When parents grow old and infirm, they may not want to burden their children with such tasks as changing their diapers or feeding them. Much better a stranger to perform these intimate tasks—a paid stranger, one with the training to reduce the patient's embarrassment over his disfunction.

One Alzheimer victim said: "Some part of my mind is a dark and dismal place. I become a different person, and I don't even know myself. I love my family, and I have such wonderful memories, but I feel I'm losing them both. I don't want them to see me like this."

Better by far for the patient to retain what tiny shred of dignity he can than to subject him to more humiliation than necessary. By and large, guilt arises when we suspect we have failed someone we love. Do the best you can for your elderly loved ones, and be brave enough to let go when you can no longer help them.

"That in me ye might have peace."
John 16:33

PREPARING FOR THE INEVITABLE

Unless we encounter an early death through sickness or accident, each of us must face the dilemma of old age. Some of us begin to prepare for it as we witness the aging processes in our parents or other loved ones. Some of us refuse to consider it as a possibility for ourselves. Those who assume the former more realistic stand are better able to deal with the problems of aging in a practical and less traumatic manner.

Are there steps that can be anticipated early in life to reduce the traumas of aging? To this question we can voice a decisive "Yes!"

All the answers, of course, are not clean-cut. In all questions dealing with human beings, individual make-up and personalities influence and reflect outcomes. Nevertheless, despite individual differences, this chapter will deal with standard issues involved in preparing for the stage in life known as "old age." Both child and parent benefit from pre-planning, before the problems become so saturated with emotion that the participants are not able to think and plan logically.

Family Support Systems

The most important aspect of preparing for old age centers around solid family ties. Even in the so-called welfare state, where social systems seem to usurp responsibilities formerly assigned to natural groupings in which people are related by blood, "families remain the most important support systems for older members."[49] And "Despite stresses and excessive demands upon their emotional and economic resources, the majority of the frail elderly are living in their own homes with support or in homes of family members."[50] The order of rank in accepting a supportive role for the old and ill falls first upon the immediate family, then upon the extended family, next upon friends, and last upon public assistance.

Of course, in actual practice, the assumption of this role depends largely on filial maturity, or the degree to which a child can accept "responsibility for his aging parent's dependency needs in a positive manner."[51] Modern society tends to regard the family according to its functions, however, and because of various sociological factors, the traditional concept of a family with father, mother, and child/children is not typical today. The "blended" family is more common with children from a previous marriage and, consequently, a stepfather or stepmother. This provides a whole new concept of extended family . . . as well as more complications. "Current linkages for the aged and their families often result in 'intimacy at a distance.' "[52] A child who has not been raised by his parent can hardly be expected to feel great sympathy for his needs when the parent grows old apart from the offspring's normal family pattern.

Be this as it may, between 1900 and 1970 life expectancy at birth increased from forty-seven years to seventy-three years, a gain of 55 percent, or twenty-six years, and it is even higher today. As statistics prove, with the explosion of the over-65 segment of the population due to increased health care and decreasing birth rates, someone has to assume support for these older citizens, many of whom find themselves with fewer children and strained or non-existent familial associations. "The family is the first and the most critical link in a continuum of . . . health services"[53] and it behooves us to form strong relationships between family members if we are to assume the rights and obligations inherent in traditional familial grouping.

Family councils, meetings in which members of a family can discuss and air mutual problems, are encouraged as a means of providing strong blood ties. All of us need to feel as if we belong, as if someone cares enough about us to be concerned about our troubles. We also need association with others who can help us integrate our past, present, and future experiences and enable us to adapt or adjust to changes in our lives. Illness, death, financial reverses, separation, depression, discouragement—all of these life experiences require the special ministrations of someone close who can sympathize, or advise, as we muddle our way along. Nothing has yet replaced the family unit for fulfilling these needs.

Positive social action forms the basis for a good self-concept, and this starts in the family. Significant turning points in life, such as graduation, marriage, birth of children, career gradations, etc., are social steps up the ladder to self-realization, and these events are most successfully shared with the family in intergenerational and interdependent futures.

If a younger member of a family grows up with the concept of an aging member as an integral part of the family, one who is experiencing changes as vital to his progress as any other family member, generally that child will appreciate and respect the aging parent or grandparent.

The negative aspects of aging are often stereotyped from prejudices gathered from isolated cases and not gleaned from factual evidence. When aging occurs within the circumference of family loyalty, each person can see the strengths as well as the infirmities of "Grandpa" and the elderly can be given his rightful portion of respect and affection without undue attention to his differences.

Families are the best providers of care for the aged because they are the closest observers of change in the older family member. They are better able to sense changes in his mental and physical health and to gain access to treatment for any changes in him that require attention. But relatives, being human, are also subject to more denial, fears, and bias than someone who is not involved emotionally with the aging citizen. In such cases, if they do not understand the changes, they should seek professional help. But professionals only supplement family resources; they do not replace them. And most professionals encourage the strengthening of natural support systems so that the family (extended as well as immediate) can carry on in the face of the loved one's decline.

Many professional, social service, and civic organizations are prepared to offer assistance to families in need of alternative aid. Geriatric day-care centers, day hospitals, senior citizen centers, and other structured facilities provide day-care or outpatient health services while the patient, most of the time, remains in the bosom of his family. Even if the elderly member lives in his own home with a child or other relative coming in periodically to provide services he can no longer perform for himself, there are auxilliary organizations to provide temporary or limited service as the need arises.

These gerontological services might include light housework, minor repairs, running errands or shopping for groceries, or perhaps more extensive benefits such as home-delivered meals, foster care, or sheltered housing. Familiarity with the availability of such facilities is essential for anyone dealing with the aged, for they can provide a necessary temporary respite, or a regular service, with which an elderly member of society can function semi-independently on his own.

Next to home care extended by the family are "programs that offer a combination of home care and day care for the elderly ill."[54] Even with these programs, the aged need support from their friends and families so that they still feel a part of the active world and the family unit. Over 2000 agencies provide home services for the ill or elderly in this country. Some states and counties, of course, are more blessed with these facilities than others, but any welfare agency, Social Security office, or Office for the Aging can assist in finding help when it is needed.

Such alternate care arrangements might include one or more of the following: live-in companion, home health aides, hospice support, Meals on Wheels, home improvement program to modify for handicaps, alternate living arrangements with various relatives, brief daily visits by a professional nurse, or hired help.

Senior citizen housing has become a large package in the quest for independent living by the elderly. In these housing complexes, often subsidized by charitable groups or, more recently, by Housing and Urban Development, the elderly find self-support groups. They often socialize, eat, and learn together yet they maintain enough privacy to insure their individuality.

General health services such as blood pressure tests, vision, and hearing screening are often provided at the site so that seniors need not travel great distances to secure them. Telephone committees, sick lists, birthday celebrations, and other special benefits assure elders that they are not alone. Usually, under these circumstances, an elderly man, or woman, can live a longer and happier life and maintain his, or her, optimum level of function.

In addition, supervised housing can make available barber/cosmetology services, handyman services, heavy cleaning services, laundry facilities, pastoral contacts, transportation, and nutritional, psychological, and medical counseling.

For those of modest income who remain in their own homes, federal programs offer funding for home renovations and maintenance at a low interest rate. Some communities sponsor work programs to encourage youngsters to perform menial tasks such as lawn mowing or snow removal for elderly citizens at a nominal hourly wage. Organizations like Boy Scouts and church groups utilize such opportunities for accruing service hours spent in performance of charitable deeds.

The Office for the Aging offers many programs and services for the older segment of the population. These programs and services include:

- Transportation
- Information and referral
- Multiservice senior centers
- Nutritional services
- In-home services
- Legal services
- Personal contact
- Complimentary card
- Outreach
- Protective services
- Safety

- Institutionally related services
- Employment
- R.S.V.P.
- Education
- Recreation
- Housing Improvement Program[55]

Other federal aids for the elderly are provided by the Veterans Administration, Social Security, and Social Service agencies. The Veterans Administration offers hospitalization for veterans as well as help with burial expenses. Social Security provides a minimal burial allowance as well as a monthly pension plan into which employers, as well as employees, have paid throughout the productive working years of the retired person. Most older citizens depend largely on this monthly stipend for their income; yet Social Security was not designed to fully support retirees, merely to supplement other pension plans. (Recent years have seen Social Security in dire fiscal straits. The future for such income from the aged seems questionable at this point.)

In addition to basic Social Security, there is a supplemental plan (SSI) for those who are handicapped or blind, although application must be made some months in advance of eligibility for receipt of such funds.

With so many of the elderly receiving Social Security income, banks have made arrangements for direct deposit of checks made out to specific persons in order to relieve the possibility of mail-box theft. And, since older people are often gullible dupes for con men, or frail victims of criminals who watch for appropriate times to rob them of their monthly income, direct deposit is a definite benefit for the elderly.

The Department of Social Services provides lunch programs at suitably located centers where seniors can gather, buses to take them there, and, often, health clinics at the same locations. Departments of Transportation offer discounts to seniors who ride the bus as do many department stores, restaurants, theaters, parks, etc., for patrons over 65.

Many oldsters with limited vision take advantage of books with large type and talking books made available by the Association for the Blind and Visually Handicapped. Similar aides are also offered for hearing impaired citizens.

Medicare and Medicaid

One area in which the aged need further help is in the whole spectrum of health care. It is estimated that the elderly pay more for health care now than they did before the Medicare and Medicaid programs began. Many of the elderly face financial ruin due to health care expenditure.[56] Americans spend 9 percent of the Gross National Product on health care, but the elderly spend as much as 30 percent. The answer seems to lie in supplementary health insurance and prepaid health care, a program known as HMO (Health Maintenance Organization).

Medicare was originally designed as a national health insurance program for the elderly. Financed by employers, by employee contributions, and by the federal government for those age 65 and over, some disabled people and those with chronic kidney failure, its intent was to enable Americans to draw on this "trust" for their health care costs when they reached age 65.

To begin with, Medicare paid about 50 percent of the average senior's total health care bill but, by 1978, Medicare paid only about 38 percent.[57] The decreasing number of physicians who would accept what Medicare paid as full and final payment led to patients being billed a greater amount, then left to collect what they could from Medicare. HMO avoids this.

The advantages of HMO are obvious. Various medical specialists practice under one roof which makes it unnecessary for an older person to travel from one part of town to another for different types of health care. Then, too, the patient can easily secure a second opinion if this is advisable. Perhaps the strongest advantage of HMO is that the patient can budget expenses and pay a certain fee each month to receive care when he needs it. So far the Social Security Administration has not given HMOs their full support, but it seems probable that they will in the near future.[58]

Medicaid is a medical assistance program for low-income people who can't afford the cost of health care. Based on income, many oldsters qualify for this program although assets as well as income are considered in determining eligibility. Medicaid is administered by the state which uses funds derived from federal and state taxes.

Many insurance companies offer supplemental Medicare and Medicaid insurance policies. Some are helpful, no doubt, but there may be a tendency for health insurance companies to appeal to the elderly on a fraudulent basis. They sometimes offer narrow and limited coverage but make it sound liberal; they make sure premiums are used up in expenses and especially profits; and they use scare tactics by declaring in no uncertain terms that present coverage is not enough.[59]

Regardless of certain accomplishments, Medicare coverage has fallen short of goals in many areas.[60] Out-of-pocket expenses that oldsters have to pay for hospitalization show a 277 percent increase between 1966 and 1978 . . . and it is undoubtedly greater now. Medicare deductible (the part that patients themselves pay) was $304 in 1983; in 1984 the deductible went up to $356. More than one half of Americans age 65 and over are now buying private insurance to supplement Medicare. Premiums for this coverage cost the elderly several billion dollars annually. (In preparing for old age, it seems we will be forced to purchase some kind of additional health insurance.)

Pre-Planned Funeral Arrangements

Almost every month advertisements urging seniors, as well as others, to make their "final arrangements" are circulated through the mail. Many of these seniors have taken advantage of one of these plans to think ahead about funeral and burial expenses and the type of service they would like to have.

Anticipating this need helps you to budget and enables you to select a plan without the coloration of deep mourning at the time of death. Some older citizens actually make these plans themselves, pay for their services on a budget plan, and by the time they die, their final expenses are already paid.

Another advantage is that prices for these arrangements are often fixed when the contract is made out. With costs escalating as they are, this is no longer a small concern.

The first time I approached a funeral director to be taken to look at caskets for my husband, I was filled with remorse. His illness was new to me and to walk into a room filled with coffins, with the thought that Frank would one day lie in one of them, was almost more than I could bear. His sons and their wives accompanied me, however, and when it came time for us to sign the papers and make a deposit, they all turned to me for the money. I was not able to consummate the deal that day, and I kept putting it off until my husband was confined to a nursing home. Then the administrator asked me to select a mortuary so that, if I couldn't be reached, they could send his remains to the place of my choice.

This directive was enough to send me to another mortuary, this time by myself. I was fortunate in that I fell into the hands of a kind professional who took me through the process of embalming, and all the business details, with great insight. I found it not at all painful. I have even written up the service, selected the location, the pall bearers, the speakers and the musicians, and entered this information on a form provided for that purpose at the mortuary. Since that time I have also provided the same services for my mother who requested that I do so. The next step is to make plans for myself. And I feel I will be able to do this with a minimum of emotional involvement since I'm an old hand at planning funerals by now.

Pre-planning a funeral service makes you aware of final expenses so that you can prepare with insurance money, or savings, or whatever is necessary to cover these costs. I suspect that many families are burdened for years to come by the final expenses for their loved ones. They naturally want to provide the best for Dad or Mom, and, deep in grief, they figure they can pay the bill somehow. They owe it to their parent to send him, or her, off in great style.

Making final arrangements for yourself, or your parent, ahead of time also eliminates bickering that sometimes accompanies emotion-fraught situations like a death in the family. If the parent has planned his own funeral, no one can reasonably object no matter what his choice might have been, especially if the deceased has already paid for it.

Legal Ramifications

Everyone should draw up a will while he is competent and able to decide the disposition of his property. If you die without a will, and your estate must be probated, nobody benefits but the lawyers, as one man put it. Court costs and legal fees will eat up whatever you might have worked to save all through your life.

In making a will it is best to consult with an attorney you trust. Wills can be drawn up without legal advice, but today's world is so complicated that a lawyer's guidance is probably a good investment.

To set up a will properly, take to the attorney's office the following:

•A complete list of real estate you own including information on location, value, and amount of mortgage still owed. Take along the deeds as well.

•A list of all other assets including bank accounts, stocks and bonds, business interests, money owed you, contracts, and valuables such as jewelry, furs or antiques.

•A list of all your debts, business and personal.

•Information on any inheritance you may receive or your right to name to whom certain properties will go after your death.

•Information on insurance policies with policy numbers, amounts, beneficiaries and any loans against them, and all pension and work benefits that might be available to your spouse or your children.

•The names, addresses, ages, and health of family members. Include information on any adopted children or if there are any impending divorces.

•Full names and addresses of anyone—or any organization—to whom you plan to leave money or property.[61]

With the preparation of a will, providing it is drawn up correctly, you should feel confident that your property will be dispersed as you wish. If you leave no will the state will take over distribution of your estate and your estate will automatically go into probate. A will that has been properly drawn up can be challenged in court, but it will be difficult to crack. On the other hand, an estate not protected by a will is vulnerable to all kinds of attacks.

Wills should state specifically who gets what, down to personal items that might cause family squabbles and bitter disputes. Generally each child should share equally in financial or property inheritances, but only after the wife, or husband, has had the use of the funds until she, or he, dies. Probably a married couple should draw up wills at the same time, specifying that "Mother and I have decided. . . ." A good lawyer will advise you of some of the pitfalls, but he will not tell you how to dispose of your assets. That is up to you.

After the will is made, it should be filed away in a safe place and reviewed every three or four years. If you move to another state, the will must be updated because states differ in their laws and your will may need minor, or even major, revisions in your new home state. "Without them, your will may be declared null and void."[62]

Trusts are often set up while retired people are still living, either to get a tax break, to provide for a continuum of the estate (and the income thereof), or to make certain their heirs do not go through the estate they have worked so hard to establish.

As soon as I realized that my husband would not be in full possession of his faculties for long, we both made out our wills and established a trust with one of his sons by a previous marriage, and myself, as trustees. Because I was also a trustor, the trust would provide for me in the event of Frank's death. And if he should survive me, it would pay his nursing home bills, funeral expenses, etc.

I felt good about our action. Frank had wanted his sons to inherit his estate, and I agreed to this before our marriage. My children were not involved in the trust. I knew my needs would be met if Frank died, and the fact that he cared enough about me to provide for me legally, touched me deeply.

There was only one hitch. The trust was not irrevocable and, in a moment of paranoia, Frank cancelled out all we had worked so hard to put together. After I made it known that he was ill . . . and convinced the lawyers handling the case that he was . . . the trust was re-established under practically the same terms. (Plus a fat legal fee.)

Other legal matters which should be resolved concern joint savings and checking accounts, and safe deposit boxes. Taxes and any legal obligations may raise their ugly heads and the bank may freeze all of the above, making them virtually closed to the survivor. There are ways to set up accounts so that the death of either husband or wife will not hamper the use of these funds at a time when the need for them may be great.

Your local banker, or a lawyer, can advise you about banking setups as well as stocks, bonds, deeds, etc., and how their ownership should be worded to give the survivor access to the funds. Again, each state differs in its laws, so your best friend may be a lawyer who is familiar with your affairs and somewhat younger than you so that he'll be around to counsel the survivor. In my case, I have chosen my accountant—a man who has worked with our finances for many years, who knows my husband's condition, and who is sympathetic to my needs. He and my youngest daughter are my joint personal representatives.

A living will—a statement declaring that the individual does not want to sustain life at all costs—gives the family, medical personnel, lawyers, clergymen, and hospitals specific directions so that the patient can control his own treatment . . . or lack of treatment. Some people do not want life-sustaining devices used on them after they have reached the point of no return, in cases such as brain death, terminal illness, or imminent death. This document supports the concept that death is preferable to prolonged suffering when that person's condition is irreversible. It also relieves the survivors, as well as the doctors and the hospital, of any responsibility for making decisions in this matter.

A standardized form to fill in may be used for this purpose along with another form to be used to donate organs after death. Both of these requests must be pre-planned and witnessed legally to be effective.

Future of Health Care

The problems of aging, and the attendant sociological, medical, and psychological implications will not simply disappear. They will remain as problems as long as there are oldsters in the land. And, according to statistics, there will be more and more old people to deal with in the coming years. An estimate states that—by the year 2000—for every one hundred people in this country, there will be eighty who are over 65.

The future speaks loudly in terms of need. In the first place, soaring health costs will necessitate a philosophic revision of our present commitments. "Can we forever afford to do everything modern science can think up?" questions Dr. Kim Bateman, immediate past president of the Utah Medical Association. "Modern society, with a commitment now to prolong life at any expense, will be faced with a major philosophical decision on future health care costs."[63] Because people are living longer, and because health care costs have increased, programs are running out of funding. If present trends continue, Medicare will be bankrupt by 1990, according to Bateman.

But after surveying a number of administrators from local nursing homes, there is perhaps no need to panic. Each of them sees funding cut or re-proportioned in other areas, not in short-changing the elderly. Nor do they see the compelling need for generations to live together as some sources suggest. Homes are not built to accommodate several different age groups under one roof, nor are they likely to be in the foreseeable future.

Still, there is a dramatic need for change in philosophy within the community. Nursing homes, for instance, will not be thought of as a place to go to die, but rather as a place to live in a quality fashion, with provisions for optimum independence and participation in community activities by the residents. Nursing homes will provide more short-term care as well as day care, under one facility, as Medicare stabilizes standard hospital and physician rates. Under the DRG (Diagnosis Related Groups) Medicare gives hospitals and physicians set rates—a low average in most cases. At this point, 48 percent of all nursing home costs are paid by private funds, 2 percent by Medicare and 50 percent by Medicare or by the state. When hospitals receive only standard rates for patients with broken legs, heart attacks, knee replacements, etc., they will be looking for another nursing care facility as quickly as the patient can be released. And, in the future, many of these patients will be rehabilitated so that they may return to their own homes, or arrange to live with relatives.

Even at the present rate, "to meet projected demands in the United States, a 100-bed facility would have to be opened every day through the year 2000."[64] Just imagine what the future will require.

Without a doubt the future will see more patients needing help, more acute care, more skilled nursing—and with the exception of a few locations—most areas in the country do not have enough beds now. It is possible that hospitals will begin to provide long-term care, because of the pressing need, although at present they are not set up to do so. Both nursing homes and other health care facilities will soon hire more registered nurses, more social workers with master's degrees, and will provide services like Meals on Wheels, home health aides, etc., to facilitate home health care.

Future emphasis will focus on both rehabilitation and support groups. Alternative care already offers sheltered housing for stroke victims and the handicapped who might otherwise find themselves in nursing homes because of lack of appropriate supervision. A new generation is finding its way into nursing homes and, consequently, staffs must provide more recreational activities, more therapy such as ceramics, handicrafts and art workshops, more educational and cultural trips, and more entertainment with an eye always open to rehabilitation.

In essence, all of us who can anticipate longer lives must learn to cope, to become more aware of possible resources for help, to become health conscious by utilizing preventive measures before we grow infirm. Furthermore, we must each take the responsibility to learn about health care, both for ourselves and for our elders, and to promote good health habits — both mental and physical — among those we contact in our daily lives.

Schools, churches, civic organizations and clubs should all make a concerted effort to educate people, to avoid the kind of denial so common today . . . the kind of denial that feels old age will never happen to us or to ours. It not only can, it will . . . and sooner than we think! "We believe that our society needs to accept aging as a natural process which we are all undergoing," says Dr. Michael Bertoch, psychologist, Utah State University. "With education on the aging process will come less fear, more ability to cope, and more pre-planning for aging. A positive attitude can do wonders, especially if it is backed by accurate knowledge! This is preventive health care."[65]

An informed electorate, along with concerned officials, will provide answers to questions in the future that we are barely beginning to formulate at the present. Meanwhile, there is no substitute for compassionate care provided for the aged, when possible, by knowledgeable and understanding families.

Whatever else the future holds for our aged, it seems certain they must look to us, their children and grandchildren, for satisfactory solutions to the problems that will eventually affect all of us. It has never been more evident that we are our brother's keeper, that he is dependent on the responsible citizens of this country to anticipate his needs in health care, housing, financial support, and general psychological and emotional well-being. Charity begins at home. Let us care for our fellowman — our parents, our ailing spouses, the elderly indigent, our progenitors — all of those who have paved the way for our bountiful lives.

The elderly can no longer be hidden away in spare rooms or in damp basement apartments with untreated medical conditions further neglected as the elderly barely subsist, day by day, on substandard diets and emotional deprivation. The aged are a vital, growing segment of our society. As such, they must be recognized and their needs met. Anything less is suggestive of the dark ages, not an enlightened civilization like ours where problems are met, head-on, and resolved.

By caring for our elders, we may be found worthy of that same compassionate treatment in our own declining years: An important consideration, for as Alex Comfort so candidly states, "The young of today are the aged of tomorrow."[66]

NOTES

Notes to Foreword

    1. Silverstone and Hyman, *You and Your Aging Parent,* jacket cover.
    2. Charles Percy, *In The Country of the Young,* 5-6.
    3. Sharon Curtain, *Nobody Ever Died of Old Age,* p. 209.
    4. Diane Rubin, *Caring, A Daughter's Story,* jacket cover.
    5. *Ibid.*

Notes to Chapter 1

    6. Bumagin and Hirn, *Aging Is A Family Affair,* p. 167-168.
    7. Dennis McFall, "Help Available for Those in Search of Care Facility," *The Herald Journal,* p. 4.
    8. Silverstone and Hyman, *op. cit.,* p. 173.
    9. *Ibid.*
    10. Percy, *op. cit.,* p. viii Preface.
    11. Curtain, *op. cit.,* back cover.
    12. *Ibid.,* p. 172.
    13. *Ibid.,* p. 173.
    14. Victor Kassel, M.D., *Deseret News,* July 29-30, 1982.
    15. Bumagin and Hirn, *op. cit.,* p. 176.

Notes to Chapter 2

    16. Mace and Rabins, *The 36-Hour Day,* p. 9.
    17. *Ibid.,* p. 25.
    18. *Ibid.,* pp. 31-32.
    19. *Ibid.,* p. 33.

Notes to Chapter 3

    20. Douglas R. Hyldahl, M.D., "Medical Professional Finds New Interest in Geriatrics," *The Herald Journal,* p. 9.
    21. Skinner and Vaughan, *Enjoy Old Age,* p. 24.
    22. Derek Cooper, "Aerobics and The Brain," *Modern Maturity,* p. 62.
    23. A. N. Exton-Smith, M.D. and D. L. Scott, M.R.C.S., *Vitamins in the Elderly,* p. 55.
    24. *Ibid.*
    25. Priscilla Eldridge, R.P.T., *Caring for the Disabled Patient, An Illustrated Guide.*
    26. James W. Long, M.D., *The Essential Guide to Prescription Drugs,* p. 806.

Notes to Chapter 4

    27. *Ibid.*
    28. *Ibid.*
    29. Peter Weaver, *Strategies for the Second Half of Life,* p. 313.
    30. *Ibid.,* p. 316.
    31. *Ibid.*

32. Percy, *op. cit.*, p. 116.
33. Weaver, *op. cit.*, p. 314.
34. William D. Poe, M.D., *The Old Person in Your Home*, p. 3.

Notes to Chapter 5
35. Weaver, *op. cit.*, p. 21.
36. *Ibid.*, 312.
37. Utah Power Utilities Newsletter, January 1984.
38. Weaver, *op. cit.*
39. Silverstone and Hyman, *op. cit.*
40. *Ibid.*, p. 205.
41. *Ibid.*
42. Curtain, *op. cit.*, p. 147.
43. Silverstone and Hyman, *op. cit.*, p. 217.
44. *Ibid.*, p. 229.

Notes to Chapter 6
45. Curtain, *op. cit.*, p. 79.
46. Weaver, *op. cit.*, 349.
47. Curtain, *op. cit.*, pp. 226-227.
48. Silverstone and Hyman, *op. cit.*, p. 185.

Notes to Chapter 7
49. Eyde and Rich, *Psychological Distress in Aging*, p. 19.
50. *Ibid.*
51. *Ibid.*, p. 16.
52. *Ibid.*, p. 14.
53. *Ibid.*, p. 1.
54. C. Carl Pegels, *Health Care and the Elderly*, p. 17.
55. *Ibid.*, p. 36.
56. *Ibid.*, p. 153.
57. *Ibid.*, p. 164.
58. *Ibid.*, p. 165.
59. *Ibid.*
60. *Ibid.*, p. 151.
61. Diane Dodson, "The Law and You," *Woman's World*, p. 7.
62. *Ibid.*
63. Tim Vitale, "Philosophy to play role in future care decisions," *Herald Journal*, p. 8.
64. Sara V. Sinclair, R.N. Administrator, Sunshine Terrace.
65. Michael Bertoch, Ph.D., Utah State University.
66. Rubin, *op. cit.*, pp. 22-23.

POSSIBLE SOURCES OF HELP

Your area Agency on Aging (see telephone directory)

Your local Social Security Office

Local Social Service Agencies (see telephone directory)

Administration on Aging
330 Independence Avenue, S.W.
Washington, D. C. 20201

National Institute on Aging
(National Institute of Health)
9000 Rockville Pike
Bethesda, Maryland 20014

Veterans Administration
"Federal Benefits for Veterans" (pamphlet)
810 Vermont Avenue, N.W.
Washington, D.C. 20420

American Association of Retired Persons
1909 K Street
Washington, D. C. 20049

National Council of Senior Citizens
1511 K Street, N.W.
Washington, D. C. 20005

National Association of Federal Employees
1533 New Hampshire Avenue, N.W.
Washington, D. C. 20036

National Council on Aging
1828 L Street, N.W. (Suite 504)
Washington, D. C. 20036

National Senior Citizens Law Center
1709 West 8th Street
Los Angeles, California 90017

Gray Panthers
3700 Chestnut street
Philadelphia, Pennsylvania 19104

American Association of Homes for the Aging
1050 17th Street, Suite 770 N.W.
Washington, D. C. 20036

BIBLIOGRAPHY

Breitung, Joan Carson, R.N. M.A. *Care of the Older Adult.* New York: The Tiresias Press, Inc., 1981.

Cooper, Derek. "Aerobics and the Brain." *Modern Maturity,* February-March 1984.

Curtain, Sharon R. *Nobody Ever Died of Old Age.* Boston: Atlantic Monthly Press, Little, Brown & Co., 1972.

Eldridge, Priscilla, R.P.T. *Caring for The Disabled Patient.* Ordell, New Jersey: Medical Economics Co., 1979.

Exton-Smith, M.D. and D. L. Scott. *Vitamins in the Elderly.* Bristol, England: John Wright & Sons, Ltd., 1968.

"How To Select A Nursing Home." U.S. Department of Health & Human Services, Baltimore, Maryland. U.S. Government Printing Office, revised since 1976.

Hyldahl, Douglas R., M.D. "Medical Professional Finds New Interest in Geriatrics." Logan, Utah: *The Herald Journal,* February 23, 1984.

Jamieson, R. H. *Exercises for The Elderly.* Verplanck, New York: Emerson Books, Inc., 1982.

Kassel, Victor, M.D. Letters to the Editor, *Deseret News,* July 29, 30, 1982.

Kreisler, Nancy and Jack Kreisler. *Catalog of Aids for the Disabled.* New York: McGraw Hill Book Co., 1982.

Kubie, Susan and Gertrude Landau. *Group Work With the Aged.* New York: International University Press, Inc., 1975.

Lindsay, Ella M., R.N. *Care of the Sick in the Home.* Salt Lake City: Bookcraft, Inc., 1975.

Long, James W., M.D. *The Essential Guide to Prescription Drugs.* Revised ed., New York: Harper & Row, 1980.

Mace, Nancy L. and Peter V. Rabins. *The 36-Hour Day.* Baltimore: The Johns Hopkins University Press, 1981.

Matthews, Joseph L. and Dorothy Matthews Berman. *Source-*

Matthews, Joseph L. and Corothy Matthews Berman. *Sourcebook for Older Americans*. Berkley: Nolo Press, 1983.

McFall, Dennis. "Help Available For Those in Search of Care Facility." Logan, Utah: *The Herald Journal*, February 23, 1984.

Nolen, William A., M.D. "The Enigma of Alzheimer's," *50 Plus*. August, 1983.

Norback, Craig and Peter Norback. *The Older American's Handbook*. New York: Van Nostrand Reinhold Co., 1977.

Percy, Charles H., Senator. *Growing Old in the Country of the Young*. New York: McGraw Hill Book Co., 1974.

Poe, William D., M.D. *The Old Person in Your Home*. New York: Charles Scribner's Sons, 1969.

Rubin, Diane, *Caring, A Daughter's Story*. New York: Holt, Rinehart & Winston, 1982.

Schmidt, Alice M., R.N. *The Homemaker's Guide to Home Nursing*. Provo, Utah: Brigham Young University Press, 1976.

Silverstone, Barbara and Helen Kandel Hyman. *You and Your Aging Parent*. New York: Pantheon Books, 1976.

Skinner, B. F. and M. E. Vaughan. *Enjoy Old Age*. New York: W. W. Norton & Co., 1983.

Tichtin, George B., M.D. *How to Be 100 Years Young*. New York: Frederick Fell Publishers, Inc., 1978.

Tobin, Sheldon S. and Mortin A. Lieberman. *Last Home for the Aged*. San Francisco: Jossey-Bass, Inc., 1976.

Weaver, Peter. *Strategies for the Second Half of Life*. New York: Franklin Watts, 1980.

Index